# THE INTERNATIONAL
# Dinner Party
# COOKBOOK
## —By Jan Bilton—

HENRY HOLT AND COMPANY   NEW YORK

Text copyright © 1985 by Jan Bilton
Photography copyright © 1985 by Endeavour Press Ltd

First published in the United States in 1986 by Henry Holt and Company, Inc.,
521 Fifth Avenue, New York, New York 10175.

Distributed in Canada by Fitzhenry and Whiteside,
195 Allstate Parkway, Markham, Ontario L3R 4T8.

Originally published in New Zealand under the title *The New Zealand Dinner
Party Cookbook*.

Library of Congress Cataloging-in-Publication Data

Bilton, Jan.
  The international dinner party cookbook.
  Includes index.
  1. Cookery, International. 2. Dinners and dining.
I. Title.
TX725.A1B516 1987     641.59     86-14321

ISBN 0-8050-0133-6

First American Edition

Designed by Sue Reidy
  Reidy-Heywood Design Partners – Auckland
Line illustrations by Sue Reidy
Artwork Production by Leonard Cobb Direction – Auckland
Photography by Rees Osborne
Typesetting by Artspec Imaging Limited Auckland
Printed and bound in Hong Kong by Everbest Printing Co. Ltd

10 9 8 7 6 5 4 3 2 1

ISBN 0-8050-0133-6

# • C O N T E N T S •

# INTRODUCTION

The secret to giving successful dinner parties is in not only presenting good food but also in making your guests feel welcome and comfortable. A warm atmosphere will stimulate conversation and pave the way to success. If guests look uncomfortable, ask them into the kitchen to help with a salad, or give them the latest photo album to discuss while you finish your preparation.

If you are new to throwing dinner parties, then start by inviting numbers your kitchen and equipment can cope with. Consider the number of plates, knives and forks available too.

Choose the menu several days in advance. Cost, number of guests and season will influence the menu. The smaller the number, the more dishes can be prepared just before serving. For large parties the more food that can be prepared in advance, the better.

Plan a shopping list and a preparation time schedule. Tables and flowers can be set the day before. Hot coffee or soup can be stored in vacuum flasks for several hours. Any last minute preparation that takes you away from your guests for more than 15 minutes, is not right for that dinner. Most importantly, allow an hour or two of relaxation before guests start arriving.

Bon appetit.

*Jan Bilton*

## SOMETHING NEW STRAWBERRY SOUP, PEPPER LAMB, HAZELNUT PIE

### STRAWBERRY SOUP

### PEPPER LAMB SKEWERS WITH RED DRAGON GLAZE

### DEEP FRIED POTATO FLOWERS

### MUSHROOMS WITH PEA PUREE

### HAZELNUT PIE

An intimate dinner for four can be fun to prepare. Not only can one experiment with new dishes with more confidence, often they can be cooked at the last minute. The more guests, the more preparation is required before hand.

Strawberry soup is a good summer dish but can also be served on colder nights — the pepper lamb following is hot! Prepare the lamb up to 12 hours ahead, cover and refrigerate. Cook just before serving.

The fried potato flowers must also be cooked just before serving.

A tossed salad can be served after the main course and before the dessert.

The hazelnut pie is rich and mellow and is best served warm with lots of whipped cream. The pastry recipe (for the Hazelnut Pie) can also be used for other pies — bake for 10 minutes if filling to be added is cold. Omit sugar if to be used for a savoury pie.

# STRAWBERRY SOUP

250g (9oz) strawberries
2 cups rosé wine
1 tablespoon lemon juice
½ cup strawberry flavoured yoghurt
½ cup cream

This rather unusual soup should be velvety smooth. Fresh or frozen berries can be used. Choose a good quality rosé wine in which to poach the berries.

Stand strawberries in wine overnight. Place in a heavy saucepan. Slowly bring to boiling point. Poach about 20 minutes until strawberries are soft and start to loose their colour. Cool.

Place fruit in a sieve, pressing berries very gently to squeeze out juice. Do not allow any of the seeds to be forced through the sieve. Add juices to wine. Chill.

Just before serving, combine yoghurt (free of seeds) and cream. Stir into strawberry liquid. Ladle into 4 soup plates.

# PEPPER LAMB SKEWERS WITH RED DRAGON GLAZE

750g (1½lb) lean, boned lamb
2 tablespoons butter, melted
freshly ground black pepper
1 tablespoon oil
1 tablespoon butter (extra)
Glaze;
3 red tamarillos or red plums
3 tablespoons sugar
½ cup water
2 tablespoons white rum

Lean lamb from the leg or fillet is cut into cubes, skewered and rolled in coarsely ground black peppers. The glaze is puréed tamarillos or plums.

Cut lamb into 3cm (1in) cubes. Thread onto 4 skewers and brush with melted butter. Roll in pepper. Refrigerate to set coating. Meanwhile prepare glaze.

Peel and halve tamarillos or plums. Place in a saucepan with sugar and water. Slowly bring to the boil and simmer until fruit is soft. Sieve. Cool until just warm then add the rum.

To cook lamb, heat oil and extra butter in a heavy frypan. Pan fry lamb 2–3 minutes each side until just cooked – lamb should be pink inside.

Place on serving plate with 2 spoonfuls of the warm glaze.

# DEEP FRIED POTATO FLOWERS

4 large potatoes
oil for deep frying

If a flower-shaped cutter is unavailable, an appropriate substitute should be chosen.

Peel potatoes and cut into 5mm (¼in) slices. Using a flower-shaped biscuit cutter, cut potato into shapes. (Boil offcuts and use for another occasion.)

To prevent flowers from discolouring, stand in salted cold water.

To cook, heat oil in a suitable saucepan or deep fryer until a bread cube will brown in 1 minute. Pat dry the potato flowers. Immerse potato in hot oil and fry until golden. Drain and serve.

# MUSHROOMS WITH PEA PUREE

8 large, firm, mushrooms
melted butter
500g (1lb) fresh or frozen green peas
3 sprigs parsley
1 teaspoon sugar
1 small potato, peeled
1 egg
salt and white pepper

Choose large mushroom caps. These may be prepared ahead and cooked at the last minute.

Snap stems from mushrooms. Brush caps with melted butter and place between 2 enamel plates or in a foil-lined steamer. Cover and cook over boiling water for 5 minutes, brushing once with butter during the cooking. Mushrooms should be firm but lightly cooked.

Meanwhile place peas in a small saucepan with parsley, sugar, chopped potato and about 2.5cm (1in) of boiling water. Cook until tender. Drain well. Blend to a fine purée in an electric blender. Cool and add beaten egg to bind.

Chill mushrooms and pea purée at this point if preparation is to be continued at a later time. Pipe purée into mushroom caps. Reheat in oven 180°C (350°F) for about 10 minutes.

# HAZELNUT PIE

**Pastry;**
75g (3oz) butter
¼ cup self-raising flour
¾ cup plain flour
⅛ teaspoon salt
1 tablespoon sugar
1 egg

**Hazelnut Filling;**
50g (2oz) butter
¾ cup firmly packed brown sugar
3 eggs
¾ cup corn or golden syrup
½ cup lightly toasted hazelnuts
2 tablespoons hazelnut liqueur
¼ teaspoon salt

Rub chopped, chilled butter into sifted flours, salt and sugar, or mix in a food processor until smooth. Add egg and gather up into a ball. If too dry, add icy water, a teaspoon at a time until dough holds together. Wrap in waxed paper and refrigerate at least 30 minutes.

To make pie shell, press pastry into a circle about 2.5cm (1in) thick. Roll out until about 5mm (¼in) thick, turning pastry 45 degrees during rolling. Line a lightly greased 18–20cm (7–8in) pie plate with the pastry. Trim edge.

For best results, chill 30 minutes. Prick base. To prevent pastry from puffing up, place a sheet of buttered foil across pastry, pressing it gently into the sides.

Bake 200°C (400°F) in centre of oven for 5 minutes, remove foil and continue baking for 3 minutes. Cool slightly before adding filling.

Lightly toast hazelnuts in oven 10 minutes at 160°C (325°F).

Cream butter and sugar until light. Beat in eggs one at a time. Add syrup, coarsely chopped nuts, liqueur and salt. Mix well and pour into pie shell.

Bake 35 minutes at 190°C (375°F) until filling is firm. Serve warm.

# CHAMPAGNE AND CHEESE FONDUE FUN

## SMOKED SALMON WITH DILL DRESSING

## CHAMPAGNE AND CHEESE FONDUE

## FRENCH BREAD AND CURRIED BREAD CUBES

## VEGETABLE GARDEN SALAD

## LIME SORBET

## MELON BALLS IN MERINGUE NESTS

Fondues originated in Switzerland and were directly related to the climate and geography of the country. The village industries of baking bread and making cheese provided a staple diet. But as winters grew colder, fresh food scarce and the cheese harder, fondues were created to make the dinners more palatable. The hard cheese was melted in wine in a communal pot and bread swirled in the cheese. Today, although there are many versions of the fondue, the principles are the same.

It is best to choose a wide, round, flat bottomed earthern ware dish that will stand firmly on top of a small spirit stove. A water-based chafing dish is also suitable. Each person should be equipped with a long handled fork. Serves four.

This is a fun meal that can be cooked at the table, and the table can be of medium size or of small coffee table dimensions, in front of the fire, or on the patio.

# SMOKED SALMON WITH DILL DRESSING

4 crisp lettuce leaves
8 thin slices smoked salmon
1 medium onion, sliced
1 tablespoon capers, drained
sprigs of fresh dill
¼ cup sour cream
¼ cup mayonnaise
2 tablespoons finely chopped
dill, or
2 tablespoons finely chopped
parsley and
1 teaspoon dill seeds
2 pitted olives, sliced

If smoked salmon is unavailable, other smoked fish may be used, such as snapper. Flake fish and arrange attractively on lettuce on a plate – continue preparations as for the salmon.

Arrange lettuce leaves on 4 small plates or shells. Top each leaf with 2 slices of salmon. Garnish with crisp sliced onions (stand sliced onions in icy water to crisp), capers, and fresh dill.

Combine sour cream, mayonnaise and seasonings. Just before serving, place a spoonful of dressing on salmon and garnish with a few slices of olive.

# CHAMPAGNE AND CHEESE FONDUE

2 cups champagne
500g (1lb) grated Swiss cheese
¼ cup flour
2 egg yolks
salt and pepper to taste
1–2 loaves French bread

Choose a dry champagne or sparkling wine. Serve a similar champagne during the meal. Use leftover egg whites to make meringue nests for the dessert.

Prepare fondue in fondue pot or in another saucepan and pour prepared finished fondue into a fondue pot.

Heat champagne slowly over low heat until nearly boiling. Toss grated cheese with flour. Gradually stir in cheese, mixing continuously until smooth. Beat egg yolks and mix into the cheese mixture. Season to taste.

Serve with French bread cut into 2.5cm (1in) cubes, and curried bread cubes. Spear bread with long fondue forks and swirl in the cheese. Vegetables may also be dipped in fondue or used as salad vegetables.

# CURRIED BREAD CUBES

half a small loaf white bread
50g (2oz) butter
2 tablespoons oil
3 teaspoons curry powder

Remove crusts from loaf and cut into 2cm (¾in) cubes.

Heat butter and oil together in a medium sized frypan – stir in curry powder.

Fry bread cubes until golden and crisp. Drain on absorbent paper. Place in a paper lined basket or bowl to serve.

# VEGETABLE GARDEN SALAD

1 green pepper
2 carrots
8 button mushrooms
8 cauliflowerettes
2 zucchini
8 cherry tomatoes
lettuce or watercress

A vinaigrette dressing can be served with the vegetables. Use seasonal vegetables.

Wash and prepare vegetables – slice pepper into 8 and remove seeds. Peel and cut carrots into sticks. Remove stems from mushrooms and peel if necessary. Blanch cauliflower for 2 minutes in boiling water then refresh in icy water. Slice zucchini in half lengthwise then in half crosswise. Blanch 1 minute in boiling water – refresh in icy water. Drain and pat dry with cauliflower. Chill. Place all vegetables with tomatoes on a platter lined with lettuce or watercress, or prepare as a nosegay.

# VINAIGRETTE

3 tablespoons white wine vinegar
salt
freshly ground black pepper
¼ teaspoon dry mustard
⅓ cup olive oil

Beat vinegar, a dash of salt, pepper and mustard with a whisk until salt dissolves. Add oil slowly whisking continuously until oil is absorbed.

# LIME SORBET

1/3 cup sugar
3/4 cup water
1/2 teaspoon powdered gelatine
2 tablespoons cold water
1/4 cup lime juice
1 drop green food colouring
1 egg white

This acts to refresh the palate after the rich fondue. Serve just a small amount in a chilled glass container, or in hollowed lime or lemon shells.

Boil sugar and water for 10 minutes. Soak gelatine in cold water then heat to dissolve. Add lime juice and colouring. Stir into sugar syrup. Cool.

Beat egg white until stiff and fold into mixture. Pour into a container and freeze until solid. Remove from freezer about 1/2 hour before serving. Garnish with mint leaves.

# MELON BALLS IN MERINGUE NESTS

2 egg whites
1/8 teaspoon cream of tartar
3/4 cup castor sugar
1 teaspoon cornflour

Meringue nests may be prepared weeks ahead. To serve, scoop balls from different colours and varieties of melon. Marinate in a little liqueur. Add to nests just before serving. Serve 1 or 2 per person.

Beat egg whites and cream of tartar until stiff. Gradually beat in sugar until smooth and satiny. Fold in cornflour.

Place mixture in a piping bag fitted with a 1cm (1/2in) tube. Cover a baking sheet with non-stick baking paper. On it draw 8, 6cm (2½in) circles. Pipe a base to each circle. Then pipe double rings of meringue on outer edges of each circle.

Bake in oven 110°C (225°F) for 1½–2 hours until completely dried out. Cool on tray then store in an airtight container.

Fill with melon balls and pass whipped cream as an accompaniment.

## A JAPANESE INFLUENCE

### ROLLED SUSHI
### SASHIMI

### TEPPANYAKI
### NOODLE SALAD
### RICE

### GREEN TEA ICE CREAM

This dinner for four has some unique flavours. In Japan, presentation of food is of utmost importance and during the last few years this has influenced the cuisine of many countries. Now, more than ever, food must look good as well as taste good.

Rolled sushi is a tasty starter and may be used as nibbles with pre-dinner drinks at any time. Vinegared rice is rolled up in seaweed or in egg wrappers. Raw fish (sashimi) is very fresh fish which is thinly sliced and eaten after dipping into ginger or soy sauce. Serve as starter number two.

The main course of teppanyaki is a mixture of meat and vegetables which can be cooked at the table and served with rice and a nutty noodle salad. Green tea makes an unusual base for the creamy iced dessert.

This meal can easily be served at a low coffee table — guests can sit on the floor on cushions. Sake is a good accompaniment to the main course. Stand the bottle in warm water before serving.

# ROLLED SUSHI

2 cups short grained rice
3 cups water
¼ cup rice wine vinegar
(or white wine vinegar)
1¼ tablespoons sugar
1 teaspoon salt

3 sheets Nori or
3 egg wrappers;
6 eggs
3 tablespoons sugar
¾ teaspoon salt
2 tablespoons chicken stock

125g (4oz) spinach
3 large mushrooms
2 carrots

This may be prepared in 2 ways. Vinegared rice and pickles can be rolled in sheets of seaweed (Nori). Egg wrappers can also be used.

To cook rice, place in a heavy pan with water. Allow to soak for about 1 hour. Cover and bring to the boil, reduce heat and just simmer for 10 minutes. Remove from heat, stand 10 minutes. All water should be absorbed by the rice.

Meanwhile combine vinegar, sugar and salt and heat until sugar is dissolved. When rice is cool, cut vinegar into the rice.

To make egg wrappers, combine eggs, sugar, salt and chicken stock — beat until sugar is dissolved. Preheat a frypan (an oblong one preferably or otherwise use a round pan and cut wrappers into oblongs after cooking and cooling). Grease pan well and pour ⅓ egg mixture into pan, tilting to swirl egg around base of pan. When egg is lightly browned, carefully turn and cook other side. Remove and place on a paper towel to absorb any excess grease.

Steam spinach until limp, squeeze out excess moisture and chop. Cut mushrooms into long strips and panfry in a teaspoon of oil until limp. Drain and pat dry. Cut carrots into julienne strips and steam until tender.

To prepare rolled sushi, place a sheet of nori or egg wrapper on a bamboo place mat or firm, clean tea towel. Spread ⅓ of the rice on the wrapper, leaving about 2.5cm (1in) each end. Working from side to side place along centre of rice, ⅓ of the spinach, then a row of mushroom then carrot. Raw fish, prawns or pickles may also be added. Pat filling gently onto the wrapper.

Lift mat up at one end and roll sushi into a firm roll — it is similar to rolling a Swiss roll. Repeat with remaining wrappers and filling. Cut into 2.5cm (1in) slices just before serving. May be prepared 12 hours ahead.

## HOW TO MAKE ROLLED SUSHI

1. Place a sheet of nori on a bamboo mat. Spread with rice and top with rows of fillings.

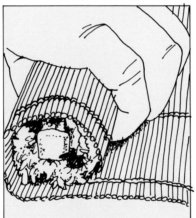

2. At one end, lift mat and roll up sushi, (see recipe instructions).

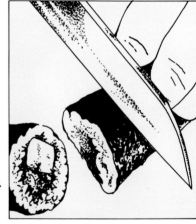

3. Cut into 2.5cm (1in) slices.

# SASHIMI

500g (1lb) fresh white fish
or tuna
salt
white vinegar
1 tablespoon finely grated fresh
ginger root
light soy sauce
2 teaspoons powdered mustard

This raw fish dish can be prepared a couple of hours in advance and refrigerated.

Salt fillets of fish lightly and stand 30 minutes. Rinse and pat dry. Remove skin and bones carefully to retain shape. Remove any discoloured parts of the fish.

Slice fish into thin, diagonal pieces, slicing from head to tail.

Dip quickly into white vinegar, shake off excess vinegar and arrange attractively on a serving plate. Serve with small balls of ginger, light soy sauce and mustard mixed to a thick paste. (See Teppanyaki for details.)

Fish is dipped into a dipping sauce and eaten.

# Teppanyaki

500g (1lb) lamb schnitzel

Marinade;
½ cup mirin (sweet sake)
or use dry sherry
½ cup light soy sauce
½ cup chicken stock

225g (8oz) prepared squid
pieces
1 large onion
1 egg plant
2 green peppers
8 mushrooms
3 cabbage leaves, finely shredded
oil

Cook at the table if possible. Beef could be used instead of lamb and vegetables in season.

Cut lamb into serving sized pieces about 6cm (2½in) square. Combine ingredients for marinade, bring to the boil, cool. Allow lamb to marinate in this mixture for several hours.

Cut squid into 5cm (2in) pieces. Slice onion into rounds about 1cm (½in) thick – push a toothpick through the centre of each onion ring to keep together. Slice eggplant into 1cm (½in) thick rounds, sprinkle with salt and stand 10 minutes. Pat dry. Quarter and de-seed the green peppers.

Remove lamb from marinade and drain well. Arrange meat and vegetables attractively on a platter.

To cook, preheat a hot plate or frypan, brush with oil. Panfry a selection of meat and vegetables until just cooked. Turn foods during cooking. The squid will take about 1 minute to cook. Serve cooked foods and refill pan with fresh food. Allow this to cook while eating. Foods can be dipped in different sauces.

Ponzu sauce; combine equal amount of lemon juice and soy sauce. Serve in small dipping saucers. Grated ginger root; peel and grate ginger root on finest part of grater. Roll into small balls. Mustard; mix powdered mustard to a thick paste in which to dip foods. Serve with small bowls of rice cooked as for the vinegared rice but do not add the vinegar mixture.

# Noodle Salad

225g (8oz) fine egg noodles
1 tablespoon sesame oil
Dressing;
6 tablespoons peanut butter
¼ cup soy sauce
3 tablespoons sesame seed paste
(tahini)
¼ cup sesame oil
1 tablespoon dry sherry
2 teaspoons cider vinegar
2 tablespoons honey
2 cloves garlic, crushed
2 teaspoons finely grated ginger
root
2–3 drops Tabasco

Garnish;
1 carrot
1 small cucumber
2 spring onions

Cook noodles in a large saucepan of boiling water until just tender. Drain and rinse under cold water to prevent further cooking. Drain well and toss in sesame oil.

To prepare dressing, combine all ingredients in a blender or food processor and mix until smooth. Thin with a little hot water if necessary.

To prepare garnish; peel carrot then continue peeling off thin strips for carrot curls. Place in icy water to curl.

Peel cucumber, halve, remove seeds by running a teaspoon down the length of the cucumber, then cut into julienne pieces. Slice spring onions diagonally.

Just before serving, toss noodles in sauce. Garnish with carrot curls, cucumber and spring onion. Prepare up to 12 hours ahead.

# Green Tea Ice Cream

2 tablespoons green tea (dry)
2 tablespoons boiling water
1 tablespoon sugar
1¼ cups milk
½ vanilla pod
2-egg yolks
¼ cup castor sugar
1¼ cups cream

This is best prepared in an ice cream maker. Soak tea in boiling water with sugar for at least 10 minutes. Place milk and vanilla pod in a small saucepan and heat slowly to boiling point. Pour over the tea and stand 5 minutes.

Beat egg yolks with castor sugar. Strain milk into the egg, cook over low heat until thickened, stirring constantly. Mixture should be thick enough to coat the back of a spoon. Chill. If desired a drop or two of green food colouring may be added to heighten the colour.

Whip cream until thick – fold into chilled tea mixture and freeze in a suitable container. If an ice cream churn is not available, freeze until mixture is slushy, beat well, then freeze until solid.

## SEAFOOD, SORREL AND SOUFFLE

### GLAZED PRAWN TARTS

### RACK OF LAMB WITH SORREL SAUCE

### POTATO WHIRLS

### SCORED ZUCCHINI

### JULIENNE OF CELERY AND PARSNIP

### RHUBARB AND RASPBERRY SOUFFLE

A *rack of lamb for six people, is baked in the oven, and is complemented by a sour sauce of sorrel. Glazed prawn tarts are served cold as a starter to the dinner — they have a thin layer of creamed salmon or tuna on the base. The raspberry and rhubarb soufflé is a light dessert but may be accompanied by sweetened whipped cream flavoured with an orange based liqueur. The colours, flavours and textures of this menu interrelate well, and the starter and dessert can be prepared several hours ahead.*

# GLAZED PRAWN TARTS

**Tartlet Pastry;**
1½ cups flour
pinch of salt
125g (4oz) butter
1 egg yolk
2–3 tablespoons iced water
**Glaze;**
1 tablespoon powdered gelatine
¾ cup chicken stock
**Filling;**
50g (2oz) cream cheese
½ cup cultured sour cream
200g (7oz) can salmon or tuna
juice ½ lemon
1 teaspoon powdered gelatine

12–18 large prawns

To make pastry, sift flour and salt. Rub in butter until mixture resembles breadcrumbs. Beat in egg yolk and sufficient iced water to hold dough together. Chill 1 hour before using. Roll out into a 23cm (9in) square. Line 6 tartlet tins with the pastry, prick base carefully and chill 1 hour. To prevent pastry from puffing up, press a square of lightly greased foil gently onto the base of the pastry. Bake 200°C (400°F) for 10 minutes, remove foil and cook a further 5 minutes. Cool.

To make glaze, soften gelatine in a little of the cold chicken stock. Add to remaining stock, bring to the boil, and dissolve — cool. Brush a little over the base of the baked tartlet cases.

To prepare filling, beat cream cheese and sour cream together until smooth. Fold in creamed salmon and lemon juice. Soften gelatine in 1 tablespoon water and dissolve over hot water. Combine with salmon mixture. Spread in a thin layer over base of each tart. Refrigerate to set.

If desired, remove shells from cooked prawns. Place 2–3 on top of each tart. Spoon a little glaze over the prawns. Allow to set in the refrigerator. Serve lightly chilled.

# RACK OF LAMB WITH SORREL SAUCE

3 racks of lamb,
3–4 chops each
2 tablespoons olive oil
salt
freshly ground black pepper
1 cup cream
1⅓ cups dry white wine
⅔ cup chopped fresh sorrel leaves
½ cup chopped fresh mint
extra mint sprigs for garnish

Racks of lamb should be chined and have skin removed.

Preheat oven to 200°C (400°F). Score fat then brush racks with oil and sprinkle with salt and pepper. Place in a baking pan and roast 35 minutes.

Meanwhile, bring cream to the boil over a moderate heat. Simmer gently, stirring occasionally, until reduced to half a cup.

Boil wine until reduced by half. Add sorrel and chopped mint and cook 2 minutes. Purée. Add reduced cream and heat through. Season with salt and pepper to taste.

Spoon 3–4 tablespoons of sauce onto each dinner plate. Arrange lamb on top. Garnish with extra mint.

## HOW TO MAKE A RACK OF LAMB

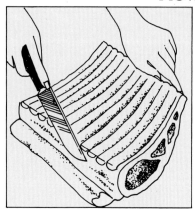

1. Ask the butcher to chine the shoulder end of the loin. Remove the chine bones.

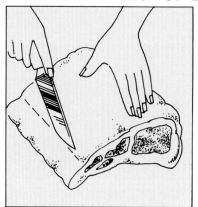

2. With bones hollow side down on a chopping board, cut a line through the flesh about ⅓ in from the thin end. Remove flank meat from top of ribs.

3. Scrape away all the flesh and meat from around the tips of the bones.

# POTATO WHIRLS

750g (1½lb) old potatoes
2 egg yolks
salt and pepper
melted butter

May be baked in advance. Store in airtight container in refrigerator. Reheat in oven, 200°C (400°F) for 4–5 minutes.

Boil peeled potatoes until soft. Drain. Mash until smooth. Add egg yolks, salt and pepper to taste.

Place potato into a piping bag fitted with a fluted tube. Pipe swirls onto a lightly greased baking tray. Brush with melted butter. Bake in a hot oven until golden.

# SCORED ZUCCHINI

6 medium zucchini

Score zucchini diagonally. Cut in half lengthwise. Steam until tender, about 5 minutes. Serve drizzled with melted butter and lemon juice.

# JULIENNE OF CELERY AND PARSNIP

400g (14oz) parsnips
6 stalks celery

Peel parsnips and cut into thin strips about 5mm (¼in) in width. Remove any coarse veins from celery and cut in a similar fashion.

Boil or steam vegetables until tender. Drizzle with melted butter and lemon juice. May be garnished with parsley.

# RHUBARB AND RASPBERRY SOUFFLE

400g (14oz) rhubarb
¾ cup water
¼ cup sugar
500g (1lb) raspberries,
fresh or frozen
3 tablespoons castor sugar
2 tablespoons powdered gelatine
2 tablespoons cold water
¾ cup hot water
2 egg whites
¼ cup sugar extra

Poach cleaned and sliced rhubarb until soft in combined water and sugar. Purée with syrup. Remove 1 cup raspberries to use for glaze. Purée remaining berries with rhubarb.

To prepare glaze, purée the 1 cup of raspberries separately. Sieve. Combine with castor sugar and cook over low heat until thick. Cool.

Soften gelatine in the cold water. Dissolve in hot water. Combine with rhubarb purée. Refrigerate until almost set.

Beat egg whites until fluffy. Gradually beat in extra sugar until stiff.

Beat fruit mixture until stiff. Fold egg whites in carefully.

Pour into a 18–20cm (7–8in) round mould, preferably with a loose base. Refrigerate until set. Spread glaze over the top. Remove from the mould onto a serving dish.

Serve with extra berries if desired.

# A MIDDLE EASTERN THEME TO DINNER

## MUSSELS WITH WHEAT

## CHICKEN WITH FETTA AND APRICOTS
## SAFFRON RICE
## MUSTARD BAKED TOMATOES
## WATERCRESS SALAD

## MARINATED GRAPES
## TURKISH DELIGHT

Cultural influences brought about by the new age of travel have encouraged the popularity of the Greek and Turkish Phylo (phyllo, filo, fila) pastry all over the world. This paper-thin flour and water pastry has some amazing applications and can be used to wrap savoury or sweet foods.

Other middle eastern influences can be seen in this menu, including the sweet-meat, Turkey's "rahat lokum", which can be served with strong black Turkish coffee in tiny cups. To make coffee in the Turkish manner, the coffee must be ground as finely as flour. To prepare 1 cup, place 2 teaspoons of coffee into a coffee pot and 1 teaspoon of sugar. Add 1 small coffee cup of water and bring to the boil, remove from heat until foam subsides, then bring to the boil again. This may be repeated 3 times. Stir and serve.

This menu is written for six guests, but may be doubled if twelve are expected.

# MUSSELS WITH WHEAT

2 tablespoons olive oil
1 large onion, diced
¾ cup kibbled wheat, washed
¼ cup sultanas or currants
½ teaspoon mixed spice
½ teaspoon salt
2¼ cups water
4–5 medium-sized mussels
per person (approx. 30)

Use a mild flavoured olive oil in this recipe. To prepare a mixture of your own, store some black olives in a small jar of safflower or sunflower seed oil – the flavour from the olives is absorbed by the oil giving it a pleasant, mild flavour.

Heat oil in a heavy frypan. Add onions and cook until soft and lightly coloured. Add currants, wheat, seasonings and 1¼ cups water. Stir until boiling. Reduce heat, cover and simmer about 20 minutes until all liquid has been absorbed by the wheat.

Meanwhile wash and scrub mussels well. Open by holding mussel firmly in one hand and cutting between the two shells, starting at the broad end. Leave shells hinged at the narrow end. Carefully pry mussel open and remove tufts from the shell.

Place about 1 tablespoon of wheat mixture in each mussel. Close shells and tie firmly with string.

Arrange mussels in a heavy saucepan – add remaining 1 cup water. Cover and steam on low heat for 20 minutes. Remove lid and allow to cool in saucepan.

Remove strings. Discard liquid. Arrange mussels in a large dish or in individual servings. Serve at room temperature or lightly chilled.

# CHICKEN WITH FETTA AND APRICOTS

3 large chicken breasts, boned
flour, salt and pepper
1 tablespoon oil
1 tablespoon butter
75g (3oz) fetta cheese
3 poached apricots, drained
12 sheets phylo pastry
oil

Sauce;
1 cup thick apricot pulp
1 tablespoon lemon juice

Apricots can be preserved or freshly cooked. Extra (cooked) apricots are required for the sauce.

Remove skin from chicken breasts. Divide each breast into 2 pieces. Toss in seasoned flour. Panfry in preheated oil and butter until lightly coloured. Remove from pan and cool. Cut a pocket in each breast and insert 2 slithers of fetta and half an apricot into each pocket.

Using 2 sheets of pastry for each piece of chicken, brush first sheet lightly with oil. Cover with second sheet and brush again with oil. Fold pastry in half crossways and brush with oil.

Place a piece of chicken in centre of one end of the pastry. Fold sides over chicken and roll up to completely enclose. Repeat with remaining chicken and phylo. (Parcels may be prepared to this point then covered and refrigerated for up to 8 hours before baking in oven.)

Place the 6 parcels on a lightly greased oven tray and brush tops with a little oil. Bake 180°C (350°F) for 10 minutes, reducing heat to 160°C (325°F) for a further 15 minutes until golden.

Meanwhile, heat apricot pulp and lemon juice gently. Serve 2–3 tablespoons over each parcel of chicken.

# SAFFRON RICE

1 tablespoon oil
1½ cups long grain rice
2 cups hot water
2 tablespoons lemon juice
2 teaspoons sugar
1 teaspoon salt
¼ teaspoon saffron threads
2 tablespoons boiling water

Cook ahead if required. Cover with plastic film and refrigerate. Reheat gently over a steamer or in microwave for about 4 minutes.

Heat oil in a heavy pan. Add rice and stir-fry 4 minutes over low heat. Add water, lemon juice, sugar and salt. Stir well, bring to boil. Cover, reducing heat to low and cook 10 minutes.

Meanwhile, pour boiling water over saffron threads and soak 5 minutes. Press strands with fingers to extract as much colour as possible.

When rice has cooked 10 minutes, lift lid and sprinkle saffron water and threads over the rice. Do not stir. Cover and cook a further 10 minutes.

Uncover and allow steam to escape for a few minutes. Toss with a fork before serving.

# MUSTARD BAKED TOMATOES

6 medium, firm tomatoes
4 tablespoons grainy mustard
¼ cup finely chopped parsley
salt and pepper

Slice tops off tomatoes. Reserve. Remove half the seeds and flesh from inside the tomatoes. Combine mustard and parsley. Sprinkle insides of tomatoes with salt and pepper. Spoon mustard mixture into the hollows.
Slice tomato tops into strips. Place on top of the mustard mixture.
Stand in a buttered baking disk and bake at 160°C (325°F) for 15 minutes.

# WATERCRESS SALAD

1 large bunch watercress
1 small buttercrunch lettuce, or
4–5 witloof (endive)
½ cup mild olive oil
3 tablespoons red wine vinegar
salt and pepper
¼ teaspoon dried tarragon
½ cup lightly toasted walnuts
6–8 black olives

Place in or on a salad bowl, the washed watercress (thick stems removed) and the lettuce or endive.
Combine oil, vinegar and seasonings. Pour over the salad and mix lightly. Scatter with nuts and olives.

# MARINATED GRAPES

2 tablespoons liquid honey
¼ cup brandy
¼ cup sweet white or
heavy red wine
6 small bunches of grapes
whipped cream or yoghurt

Dissolve honey in brandy and wine. Soak grapes in this marinade for several hours. Serve in individual glasses accompanied by cream or yoghurt.

# TURKISH DELIGHT

2 tablespoons powdered gelatine
¾ cup cold water
2 cups sugar
1 cup boiling water
½ teaspoon citric acid
few drops rosewater
few drops red food colouring
200g (7oz) semi-sweet chocolate
1 teaspoon vegetable shortening

Serve drizzled with melted chocolate.
Soften gelatine in cold water. Add sugar and boiling water. Stir over medium heat until boiling. Boil 15 minutes, stirring occasionally. Remove from heat and add citric acid, rosewater and colouring. Pour into a 20cm (8in) mould or tin and allow to set in refrigerator for at least 24 hours. Cut into diamonds.
Melt chocolate and shortening in a small bowl over hot water (or in microwave 2 minutes). Allow to cool, but while still liquid, drizzle over Turkish Delight in a lacy pattern. (Alternatively, candy can also be tossed in a mixture of equal parts icing sugar and cornflour, then served.) Serve with coffee.

# INDIA'S INTERESTING FOOD

## SAMOSA

## SPICY FRIED FISH
## TANDORI CHICKEN ON SALAT
## SPINACH RAYTA
## CHAPATIS
## RICE

## BARFI (SWEETMEAT)

This dinner party is for six people.

The spices that are an essential part of Indian food such as black mustard seeds, cumin seeds and fenugreek can be purchased quite reasonably from specialty stores. Keep in airtight containers to retain a good flavour. The meal commences with little pastries filled with spicy potato — they are deep fried. They can be prepared ahead and reheated in an oven.

The spicy fried fish (or tali machi) can be cubed ahead of time and the batter prepared — it must be deep fried just before serving. Pickles or chutneys can be served as accompaniments. The red chicken is served on a plate of salat (salad) and should be marinated overnight for best results.

Spinach Rayta is good to serve at any time. Other vegetable dishes such as chopped cucumber, or fruits such as diced tamarillos, kiwifruit and bananas, can complement the spicy foods. Traditionally, Indian meals are served in small bowls on individual guest trays.

Boiled rice (see pg 41) can also accompany the meal along with the Indian bread, chapatis.

# SAMOSA

18 spring roll wrappers

Potato filling:
225g (8oz) potato
1 tablespoon oil
½ teaspoon black mustard seeds
2 teaspoons grated ginger root
1 small onion, diced
½ teaspoon each cumin,
fennel seeds
¼ teaspoon turmeric
½ cup peas, fresh or frozen
¼ teaspoon salt
½ teaspoon garam masala
dash cayenne pepper

oil for deep frying

Filling can be of minced steak or lamb or potato. Precook meat with seasonings in a similar way to the potato.

Spring roll wrappers should be cut into 6cm (2½in) strips. To make filling, boil peeled potatoes until just tender. Drain and cut into 1cm (½in) cubes.

Heat oil in a large heavy frypan. Add mustard seeds and cook until they begin to pop. Add ginger and onions and stir fry for about 6 minutes until golden. Stir in fennel, cumin, turmeric, blanched peas and salt. Reduce heat to low, cover pan and cook for 10 minutes. Remove from heat and stir into the potato, masala and pepper. Cool before using.

Place a teaspoon of the filling at one end of the wrapper and fold pastry over diagonally, then continue folding over and over again. Keep a triangle shape. Moisten end with water and seal lightly.

To cook, heat oil in a deep pan until a faint haze rises. Deep fry samosa, a few at a time, until golden. Drain on absorbent paper. Serve warm with pre-dinner drinks.

# SPICY FRIED FISH

Batter:
½ cup chick pea flour
¼ cup rice flour
½ teaspoon each ground cumin,
cayenne, salt
¼–½ cup cold water

500g (1lb) sole fillets, skinned
1 teaspoon salt
oil for deep frying
1 onion, thinly sliced
1 large fresh or canned chilli
¼ teaspoon garam masala

Usually this TALI MACHLI requires sole fillets but other firm white fish can be used (orange roughy is good).

To prepare batter, combine flours and seasonings with enough water to mix to a smooth batter thick enough to coat the back of a spoon.

Prepare fish by rinsing in cold water — pat dry. Cut each fillet in half lengthways then each half into 6 pieces. Sprinkle with salt.

Drop fish into batter and turn to coat. Deep fry in oil (temperature 180°C or 350°F) 4–5 pieces at once. Remove when golden. Drain on absorbent paper and keep warm in a warm oven. Repeat until all the fish is cooked.

To serve, place fish on serving plate and top with onion, diced chilli and sprinkle with garam masala.

# TANDORI CHICKEN

1x1.5kg (3lb) chicken
1 teaspoon ground saffron
or turmeric
1 tablespoon boiling water
⅓ cup lemon juice
1 tablespoon salt
1 teaspoon each coriander and
cumin seeds
1 tablespoon grated fresh ginger
root
2 cloves garlic, chopped
¾ cup plain yoghurt
few drops red food colouring
¼ teaspoon cayenne

Substitute saffron threads for powdered saffron if available.

Pat chicken dry inside and out. Truss. Cut a slit between thigh and body of bird.

Dissolve saffron in boiling water. Combine lemon juice and salt and rub over bird pressing into the slits. Stand in a casserole. Brush with saffron mixture. Stand 30 minutes.

Toast coriander and cumin seeds in a small heavy frypan 1 minute, stirring. Place in an electric blender with ginger, garlic and a little of the yoghurt. Blend until smooth. Add to remaining yoghurt. Add food colouring and cayenne, mix well and spread over the chicken. Cover and marinate overnight.

Place chicken on a rack in an oven pan. Bake 180°C (350°F) for 1½ hours turning and basting once during cooking.

Remove trussing. Cut chicken into 6 serving pieces and place on a platter of salat.

# SALAT

2 medium onions
2 large tomatoes
6 radishes
2 lemons
3 chillies, fresh or canned
3 tablespoons lemon juice
½ teaspoon salt
freshly ground black pepper

Peel and halve onions lengthways. Slice very thinly. Place over the base of the serving platter (for the chicken). Place tomato rings around outside edge, with radishes, lemon wedges and chillies.

Sprinkle vegetables with lemon juice, salt and pepper.

Serve topped with the Tandori chicken.

# SPINACH RAYTA

500g (1lb) spinach
1 tablespoon oil
1 teaspoon black mustard seed
1 teaspoon whole cumin seeds
1 teaspoon ground cumin
½ teaspoon fenugreek seeds
pinch cayenne
salt to taste
½ cup plain yoghurt

Prepare this vegetable dish several hours ahead and serve at room temperature.

Wash spinach and remove thick stalks. Chop coarsely and steam in a saucepan for 5 minutes until wilted. Drain well, squeezing out excess moisture.

Heat oil in a small frypan and fry mustard seeds until they begin to pop. Add other seeds and stir fry until golden. Remove from heat, add cayenne and salt. Cool. Add to the yoghurt and stir into spinach.

# CHAPATIS

1½ cups wholemeal flour
½ teaspoon salt
1 tablespoon oil
½ cup warm water

This bread may be prepared ahead and frozen if need be. To eat, tear off a piece of 'bread' and enclose in it some of the accompaniments to the meal.

Reserve ¼ cup flour for rolling – place remaining in a bowl with salt and oil. Mix to a firm dough with water and knead on a lightly floured surface for 10 minutes. (Or use dough hook in mixer or food processor for kneading – use all the flour.)

Roll into a ball, wrap in waxed paper and refrigerate for 30 minutes.

Shape into balls about the size of a walnut. Roll out thinly (as for a French crêpe). Fry one at a time on a lightly greased heavy pan. Cook each side about 1 minute, pressing around edges with a fish slice to encourage chapati to bubble in the centre. Makes about 12.

# BARFI (SWEETMEAT)

1 tablespoon ghee
3 cups milk
1 cup sugar
75g (3oz) ground almonds
150g (5oz) ground pistachio nuts
2 drops almond essence

An almond flavoured sweetmeat which can be served after dinner with fresh mangoes and/or tea.

Brush softened ghee over a 20cm (8in) pie dish.

Bring milk to the boil in a heavy based, large, saucepan. Reduce heat to moderate and simmer 35–40 minutes until milk is the consistency of thick cream. Add sugar and stir slowly on low heat for 10 minutes.

Add nuts and cook for 5 minutes, stirring, until mixture is thick enough to come away from the sides of the pan.

Remove from heat and add essence. Pour into tin. Cool, refrigerate. Cut into diamond shapes when firm.

## TRADITIONAL FRENCH IMPRESSIVE

## RIS DE VEAU GRATINE

## FILLET DE BOEUF BOUQUETIERE

## BAVAROIS RUBANE

*Stylish French cuisine always appeals to guests and is an interesting challenge to serve. The recipes presented here are traditionally based rather than in the 'nouveau' style.*

*Ris de veau gratiné are sweetbreads lightly covered in a cream sauce and a little cheese and then grilled. It is a dish that may be prepared ahead and grilled just before serving.*

*The beef fillet is so called because of the garnish of artichokes filled with carrot and turnip balls, dice of French beans, peas, and cauliflower coated in Hollandaise sauce. The beef and vegetables can be prepared ahead but must be cooked just before serving. Small château (olive shaped) potatoes are also served.*

*The dessert is a colourful array of fruit purées in a mould. The purées are combined with a creamy custard and bonded with gelatine, and may be prepared a day or two in advance or even deep frozen for up to 1 month. These recipes serve six.*

# RIS DE VEAU GRATINE

750g (1½lb) sweetbreads
2 tablespoons each finely
chopped carrots, onions, celery
and ham
50g (2oz) butter
bouquet garni
⅛ teaspoon salt
dash of pepper

Sauce;
2 tablespoons butter
2 tablespoons flour
¾ cup cream
½ teaspoon lemon juice
salt and pepper

Topping;
⅓ cup finely grated Swiss cheese

To prepare sweetbreads, wash well then soak in cold water for 4 hours. Change water every hour. Peel off any filament. Trim.

Sauté vegetables in butter with bouquet garni (a parsley sprig, thyme and bayleaf), salt and pepper, for about 10 minutes until tender.

Arrange sweetbreads in frypan and baste with vegetables and butter. Cover and cook gently for 5 minutes. Turn, baste and cook a further 5 minutes. Reserve any juice that forms. Transfer mixture to 6 individual fireproof dishes.

To make sauce, melt butter in a saucepan and stir in flour, cooking 1 minute. Whisk in reserved juices and simmer 1 minute. Slowly whisk in cream, bring to the boil, stirring — add a little more cream if sauce is too thick. Season with lemon juice, salt and pepper. Spoon over the sweetbreads. Sprinkle with cheese. Leave to one side until ready to serve.

To cook, place about 10cm (4in) under a pre-heated grill and heat for 10 minutes until sweetbreads are heated through and the top of the sauce is browned.

# FILLET DE BOEUF BOUQUETIERE

1.2kg (2½lb) centre cut fillet of beef
1 tablespoon salt
½ teaspoon freshly ground black pepper
2 tablespoons butter

Trim meat and tie at equal intervals in 4 places round the meat. Sprinkle with salt and pepper and rub softened butter into all sides of meat. Place meat on a rack in an oven pan.

Preheat oven 220°C (425°F). Meat will take about 30 minutes to cook — have accompaniments prepared and ready to serve at the same time.

# ARTICHOKES

6 globe artichoke bottoms
½ cup carrot balls
½ cup turnip balls
50g (2oz) butter

To cook globe artichokes, trim about 2.5cm (1in) from top. Place in a large saucepan of boiling salted water to which a tablespoon of lemon juice has been added. Boil 20–25 minutes, until a leaf comes away from the side easily. Drain well. Remove leaves from top until a base is formed. Keep warm.

Meanwhile, using a small melon baller prepare carrot and turnip balls. Braise in butter in a heavy pan until just tender. Served piled in centre of artichokes.

# FRENCH BEANS AND PEAS

500g (1lb) French beans
400g (14oz) peas
2 tablespoons butter

Dice beans and mix with peas. Boil in 2cm (¾in) water with ½ teaspoon salt and sugar. Drain when cooked, return saucepan to element (with vegetables) to evaporate excess moisture. Mix with butter, tossing vegetables to coat well.

# CAULIFLOWER WITH HOLLANDAISE SAUCE

6 medium cauliflowerettes

Hollandaise sauce;
2 egg yolks
1 tablespoon lemon juice
¼ teaspoon salt
150g (5oz) butter, melted

Steam cauliflower until just tender.

To make sauce in an electric blender, combine egg yolks, lemon juice and salt in the blender. With motor running, pour in melted butter in a thin stream. Keep sauce warm by standing container in warm water.

To serve, coat cauliflower evenly with sauce.

# CHATEAU POTATOES

750g (1½lb) potatoes
50g (2oz) butter

Peel potatoes and shape into ovals about the same size as a small egg. Plunge into boiling water for 2 minutes. Drain well. In a heavy saucepan melt the butter. Add potatoes and sauté until golden, turning often. Alternatively, they may be roasted in the oven for about 10 minutes.

# BAVAROIS RUBANE

3 egg yolks
¼ cup sugar
1 teaspoon cornflour
¾ cup boiling milk
1 tablespoon gelatine
¼ cup orange juice
3 egg whites
1 tablespoon castor sugar
½ cup cream, whipped
½ cup raspberry purée
½ cup strawberry purée
½ cup apricot purée

Use fresh, or frozen and thawed berries, and cooked apricots.

Prepare a custard by whisking egg yolks with sugar until pale. Beat in the cornflour. Slowly pour in the milk, beating continuously. Cook over a low heat or in a double boiler until mixture is thick enough to coat the back of a spoon.

Dissolve gelatine in warm orange juice. Stir into the custard.

Beat egg whites, slowly adding sugar until stiff and satiny. Fold into the hot custard. Chill until syrupy.

Whip cream and fold into custard. Divide into 3 equal amounts. Fold 1 fruit pureé into each custard. Pour one into a 1 litre (1 quart) mould and set in the refrigerator. Pour next purée and custard mixture on top and allow to set. Repeat with remaining mixture. Place a piece of waxed paper over the top. Refrigerate until firm. This can be prepared a day in advance.

To unmould, stand mould in warm water. Reverse onto a chilled serving plate. Garnish with fresh berries.

# A VEGETARIAN DINNER

## MUSHROOM PATE

## THREE COLOUR CANNELLONI
## CALDWELL SALAD
## CARROT AND WHEATGERM MUFFINS

## FEIJOA SORBET WITH HONEY BANANAS

A *no-meat, full-of-flavour, dinner for six. The pâté is a combination of ground almonds and mushrooms and looks very* like a traditional pâté. Prepare the day before and keep covered in the refrigerator.

The cannelloni has two different fillings, cottage cheese and spinach, and is Pre- served tomato on a bed of concassée. pare ahead and reheat in oven. The zucchini and apple salad flavoured with basil is a complement to the pasta. Wholesome muffins are a different bread accompaniment.

Feijoas are known as pineapple quavas in some parts of the world. If fresh or canned fruit are not available, then pineapple, papaya or apricot sorbet also goes well with the honey bananas.

# MUSHROOM PATE

50g (2oz) butter
1 small onion, chopped
1 clove garlic, crushed
400g (14oz) mushrooms,
chopped
¾ teaspoon salt
dash white pepper
¼ teaspoon dried thyme
¾ cup ground almonds
2 tablespoons oil

Melt butter in a large frypan and add onion, garlic, mushrooms, salt, pepper and thyme. Cook over medium heat, stirring occasionally, until vegetables are soft and juice has evaporated.

With motor of blender running, add mushroom mixture to almonds and oil and blend until smooth. Pack into a small loaf pan or crock and refrigerate until set.

Serve sliced with buttered fingers of toast and gherkins.

# THREE COLOUR CANNELLONI

12 tubes cannelloni
500g (1lb) spinach
¼ teaspoon tarragon
¼ cup fresh breadcrumbs
500g (1lb) cottage cheese
¼ cup cream
dash nutmeg
1 egg, beaten
450g (15oz) can tomatoes
½ teaspoon dried oregano
1 teaspoon sugar
salt and pepper
1 cup sour cream
parmesan cheese

Prepare cannelloni according to manufacturer's instructions. Fresh cannelloni needs only to be filled, or use strips of fresh pasta cut about 8x10cm (3x4in). Some dried pasta may be filled directly without pre-cooking.

Wash, chop and steam spinach until cooked. Drain and squeeze out excess moisture. Chop finely and add tarragon and breadcrumbs. Mix until well combined.

Combine cheese, cream, nutmeg and egg, beating until well combined.

Mash tomatoes and simmer with seasonings until thick. Beat sour cream until smooth.

Fill 6 cannelloni with the spinach filling and the remaining 6 with the cottage cheese mixture. Place in a single layer in a well greased oblong baking dish. Spoon over the sour cream evenly and sprinkle with parmesan cheese. Bake about 30 minutes at 180°C (350°F). If top needs browning quickly place under a hot grill.

Spread a couple of spoonfuls of tomato on base of serving dish and place 2 tubes cannelloni on top (1 of each type).

# CALDWELL SALAD

¼ cup salad oil
3 tablespoons white wine vinegar
1 teaspoon basil
¼ cup chopped parsley
1 teaspoon sugar
salt and pepper
3 crisp, green skinned apples
1 small onion, diced
500g (1lb) zucchini, thinly sliced

An unusual combination of apples and zucchini.

Combine oil, vinegar, sugar, basil, parsley, salt and pepper in a large salad bowl.

Core and dice apples and toss in dressing. Add onion and zucchini. Cover and chill. Just before serving mix salad well.

# CARROT AND WHEATGERM MUFFINS

50g (2oz) butter
¼ cup firmly packed brown sugar
2 eggs
1 tablespoon lemon juice
1 tablespoon water
1 cup finely grated carrot
1 cup flour
2 teaspoons baking powder
½ teaspoon salt
¼ teaspoon ground ginger
2 tablespoons wheatgerm

Prepare ahead and warm briefly in the oven or in microwave for 15 seconds per muffin.

Cream butter and sugar until light. Add eggs and whip until fluffy. Add lemon juice, water and carrot.

Combine, sifted flour, baking powder, salt, and ginger with wheatgerm and mix into the carrot. Stir until ingredients are just moistened.

Spoon into lightly greased muffin tins, filling about ⅔ full.

Bake 200°C (400°F) for 12–15 minutes until golden. Makes 8–10 muffins. Recipe may be doubled if required.

# FEIJOA SORBET

¾ cup sugar
2 cups water
grated rind and juice of 1 lemon
2 cups pulped feijoas

Use fresh poached or canned feijoas.

Dissolve sugar in water, add rind and juice.

If fruit is fresh peel thinly and slice into syrup – poach until tender. Remove fruit with a slotted spoon and purée. Meanwhile, boil syrup steadily for 10 minutes. Chill.

If using sweetened, canned fruit, 2 tablespoons of sugar may be removed from the ¾ cup measure.

Combine equal amounts of cold sugar syrup and fruit purée. Place in the freezer in a suitable container. Freeze until almost solid, beat well then freeze until hard.

To serve, stand at room temperature for 5 minutes before scooping into individual dishes containing honeyed bananas.

# HONEY BANANAS

4 medium bananas
juice of 1 lemon and 1 orange
3 tablespoons honey
freshly grated nutmeg

Peel bananas and slice into a bowl. Combine fruit juice and honey and pour over the fruit making sure it is well coated.

Place in the base of a serving dish and top with scoops of sorbet and freshly grated nutmeg.

# CHINESE FOR SIX

## CORN SOUP
## CHILLI PRAWNS

## STEAMED PEARL BALLS
## RED ROASTED DUCK
## HOT CUCUMBER IN SESAME OIL
## GINGERED CABBAGE
## RICE

## MELON BASKET SALAD

The general rule when serving Chinese is to prepare small but different dishes for each person. A meat, fish and poultry recipe is usually chosen with vegetable accompaniments. Each dish is placed in the centre of the table and shared. As many dishes are stir fried, this involves the chef in much last minute preparation. The menu here is not traditional in that there are many different cookery methods involved. But it is a menu that the chef can enjoy together with the guests.

For extra vegetables serve the duck with watercress. Small bowls of Chinese pickles are always popular. Serve Chinese tea (jasmine is good) during the meal.

Desserts are not usually part of a Chinese meal but fresh fruit in a melon is a refreshing end.

# CORN SOUP

4 cups chicken stock
3 slices fresh ginger root
450g (15oz) can creamed corn
1 tablespoon cornflour
2 tablespoons water
125g (4oz) can crab meat
2 egg whites, lightly beaten
salt to taste

In a heavy saucepan, combine chicken stock and ginger – simmer 1 minute. Add corn, stirring well, and bring to the boil. (If a smoother soup is required, it may be puréed in the blender.)

Stir in cornflour which has been mixed to a paste with the water. Heat soup until thick and clear. Flake crabmeat and add. Remove from heat and pour in egg whites all at once. Serve in small bowls during the meal.

# STEAMED PEARL BALLS

½ cup short grained rice
500g (1lb) lean pork mince
1 egg
2 teaspoons soy sauce
1 teaspoon salt
4 mushrooms
6 water chestnuts (canned)
1 teaspoon finely chopped
ginger root
1 spring onion, diced

Balls of seasoned pork are spiked with rice.

Cover rice with 1 cup cold water and soak for 2 hours. Drain then spread on a cloth to dry.

Combine pork, lightly beaten egg, soy sauce, salt. Mix well. Then add finely chopped mushrooms and chestnuts, ginger, and spring onions and mix well.

Roll mixture into balls about the size of walnuts. Roll one ball at a time in the rice, pressing gently so rice adheres to meat. Stand balls on waxed paper.

Place a piece of waxed paper loosely on the base of a steamer. Arrange pork balls on the paper. Cover and steam over boiling water for 30 minutes. Serve at once.

# CHILLI PRAWNS

500g (1lb) large prawns
1 tablespoon finely chopped
ginger root
1 large clove garlic, crushed
3 spring onions, diced
2 chillies, chopped finely
1 tablespoon dry sherry
2 tablespoons soy sauce
1 teaspoon sugar
¼ teaspoon salt
1 tablespoon tomato paste
1 tablespoon cornflour
2 tablespoons chicken stock
2 tablespoons oil

Use green prawns preferably.

Remove shells and veins from prawns if necessary. Wash and pat dry. Have all ingredients prepared and ready to use.

Heat oil in a large wok or frypan over high heat. Add ginger, garlic, onions and chillies and stir-fry 30 seconds. Add prawns and stir-fry 2 minutes until prawns turn pink.

Add sherry, soy sauce, tomato paste, sugar and salt, stirring. Combine cornflour with chicken stock and stir into pan until mixture thickens. Transfer to a heated bowl and serve immediately.

# RED ROASTED DUCK

1 medium sized duck
1 tablespoon salt
1 bunch parsley
4 spring onions, chopped coarsely
1 tablespoon freshly ground
black pepper
2 tablespoons grated fresh
ginger root
½ teaspoon five spice powder
1 tablespoon honey
1 tablespoon dry sherry
2 teaspoons sesame oil
1 tablespoon soy sauce
½ teaspoon red food colouring

Duckling can be served with flesh cut into 5cm (2in) squares and replaced in original position on duck.

Remove neck and giblets from body cavity. Dry with paper towels. Rub with salt. Place parsley and onions into body cavity. Truss duck securely with string.

Combine remaining ingredients. Brush mixture over duck. Wrap in foil and refrigerate for at least 4 hours.

Half fill a roasting pan with hot water. Place a rack in the pan – the water should not reach the rack. Place duck on the rack, breast side up.

Roast 180°C (350°F) for 30 minutes, cover with foil and cook a further 30 minutes. Turn duck breast side down, cook 30 minutes. Remove foil during last 15 minutes of cooking.

# HOT CUCUMBER IN SESAME OIL

2 medium cucumbers
1 teaspoon salt
4 tablespoons sesame oil
1 teaspoon peppercorns
1 tablespoon sugar
¼ cup white vinegar
2 tablespoons soy sauce
1 teaspoon cornflour
2 tablespoons water
2 spring onions, sliced diagonally
1 clove garlic, crushed

Peel cucumber and rub with salt. Rinse and pat dry. Cut lengthwise and remove seeds. Cut into sticks about 5cm (2in) long.

Heat oil in a heavy pan, add peppercorns and fry for a few seconds. Stir in sugar, vinegar, soy sauce, and cornflour mixed with water. Bring to the boil. Add onions, garlic and cucumber. Cover pan and simmer 2–3 minutes until cucumber is crisp–tender. Serve warm or at room temperature.

# GINGERED CABBAGE

225g (8oz) cabbage
(Chinese if possible)
1 tablespoon salt
4cm (1½in) piece ginger root
2 tablespoons oil
¼ cup vinegar
1 tablespoon sugar
¼ teaspoon chilli powder

This dish can be prepared 2 days in advance – it is served cold.

Wash cabbage leaves well and cut into 5cm (2in) squares. Place in a glass or pottery bowl and sprinkle with salt. Stand 3–4 hours. Peel and finely shred the ginger and add to cabbage.

Heat oil in a small pan until just warm and add vinegar, sugar and chilli powder. Pour over the cabbage and stand another 3–4 hours. Keep in the refrigerator covered with plastic film.

# RICE

2 cups long grain rice
3 litres water
2 teaspoons salt

This method produces a fluffy rice.

Rinse rice in a sieve under cold water tap. Drain. Bring water to boil in a large saucepan and add salt. Slowly add rice. Boil rapidly (uncovered) for about 20 minutes, until rice is tender. Stir once or twice.

Turn into a sieve and wash under hot water tap. Drain. Stand over simmering water until required (in sieve or steamer). Fluff with a fork before serving.

# MELON BASKET SALAD

1 medium watermelon
450g (15oz) can lychees, drained
8–10 loquats or kumquats
(canned)
4 kiwifruit
8 watermelon balls
2 oranges, segmented
8 strawberries
small bunch grapes
6 pieces crystallised ginger sliced
ginger wine (optional)

Other seasonal fruits may be used as required. Rock or honeydew melons are suitable for individual servings.

Cut melon in half leaving a 2.5cm (1in) half circle (handle) attached in the centre (see illustration). Scoop out flesh. Keep flesh as whole as possible and prepare melon balls with a melon baller.

Just before serving place fruit in melon, sprinkle with ginger and a little ginger wine if desired. Serve on to small plates with tiny forks or cocktail sticks.

## HOW TO MAKE A MELON BASKET

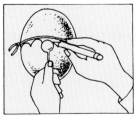
1. Using a melon baller cut around centre of melon.

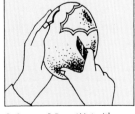
2. Leave 2.5cm (1in) either side for a handle.

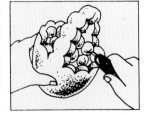
3. Remove flesh from under handle and inside basket.

## THE GOOD THINGS IN LIFE

### MOUSSELINE OF SEAFOOD

### DUCK WITH GREEN PEPPERCORN SAUCE
### PANNED SWEET POTATOES
### BEAN BUNCHES
### SPRING SALAD

### CHOCOLATE CREPES WITH PORT STRAWBERRIES

The title says it all!

Eight individual moulds of seafood mousseline can be attractively garnished with julienne vegetables or herbs. They are served chilled, therefore can be prepared a day in advance.

Duck usually appears to be all bone but this recipe calls for removal of any obvious bones — it is pre-roasted with honey then reheated with a peppercorn sauce just before serving. To complement it, there is a dish of very sweet potatoes and little bunches of fresh beans with lemon butter. There is limited use of the oven in this menu.

The chocolate crêpes are delicious when filled with liqueur-soaked fruits — choose whatever is in season. To freeze the crêpe, see the instructions in the recipe.

# MOUSSELINE OF SEAFOOD

*Velouté sauce;*
*3 tablespoons butter*
*3 tablespoons flour*
*3 cups chicken or fish stock*
*pinch nutmeg*

*1½ tablespoons gelatine*
*¼ cup water*
*750g (1½lb) cooked seafood*
*¾ cup cream*

A mixture of seafood can be used such as equal amounts of white fish and scallops or crayfish (or lobster). Individual servings can be prepared or the mixture may be set in a ring mould.

Prepare sauce by melting butter over low heat in a heavy pan (not aluminium as it may discolour the mixture). Blend in flour and gradually add chicken stock, cooking and stirring until thick.

Place over hot water and simmer gently for 45 minutes, stirring occasionally. Strain. Season. About 2¼ cups of sauce should be prepared. Add gelatine which has been soaked in water. Cool mixture.

Meanwhile, chop seafood finely or place in food processor and chop briefly. Add to cooled sauce. Whip cream until it forms soft peaks. Fold into mixture. Season if necessary. Spoon mixture into 8 individual moulds (or 1 large) which have been rinsed in cold water. Chill until firm. Unmould onto serving plates. Garnish with dill, julienne vegetables and lemon.

# DUCK WITH GREEN PEPPERCORN SAUCE

*2–3 ducks*
*½ cup liquid honey*
*½ cup cognac*
*1 cup white wine*
*1 cup chicken or duck stock*
*3 tablespoons green peppercorns*

Two large ducks or 3 medium will serve about 8. Remove rib cage bones and thigh bones, anything that will make duck eating easier. Use a sharp boning knife for best results.

Remove giblets from duck. (Bones and giblets can be used to make stock.) Cut each duck into 4–6 serving pieces, removing as many bones as possible but keeping a good shape. Brush pieces with warmed honey and place in a roasting pan. Bake 200°C (400°F) for 30 minutes, turning once during cooking and brushing again with honey. Cool and refrigerate until ready to serve.

Meanwhile, combine cognac, wine and stock and simmer until reduced by half. Cool.

Before serving, spoon the sauce over the duck and reheat 180°C (350°F) for 20 minutes, lightly covered. Add rinsed peppercorns and continue cooking 10 minutes. A small pastry duck can be used as a garnish.

## HOW TO JOINT A DUCK

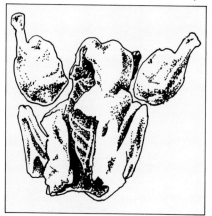

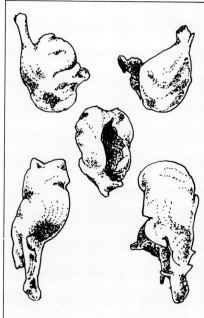

1. Remove giblets from duck. A duck can be cut into 4–6 serving pieces depending on size.

2. Cut off legs by pressing out and down. Cut between leg and body through skin and flesh.

3. Snap off at the joint.

4. Cut at an angle through the carcass to separate breasts from the backbone.

5. Cut breasts in two lengthways.

6. With a sharp boning knife, remove as many bones as possible. Fold duck portions into a good shape.

# PANNED SWEET POTATOES

| | |
|---|---|
| 6 medium kumara (or sweet potato) 50g (2oz) butter grated rind and juice of 1 orange ½ cup brown sugar ¼ cup finely chopped parsley | Boil peeled kumara in salted water until just tender. Slice into 2cm (¾in) pieces. In a large heavy frypan (a non-stick pan is good), melt butter. Add potatoes, orange rind and juice and brown sugar. Shake potatoes and cook until heated through, turning once. Garnish with parsley. |

# BEAN BUNCHES

| | |
|---|---|
| 1kg (2lb) fresh beans 1 teaspoon salt 1 teaspoon sugar 50g (2oz) butter, melted 2 tablespoons lemon juice | Trim beans and cut into approximately 10cm (4in) lengths (more or less depending on the type of bean). Push through a bean slicer. Tie in 8 bundles with a strip of bean or a circle of red or green pepper. Place in a steamer – cook just before serving. Sprinkle with salt and sugar and steam about 10 minutes or until just tender. Serve drizzled with butter combined with lemon juice. |

# SPRING SALAD

| | |
|---|---|
| 1 large lettuce 8 spring onions watercress croûtons vinaigrette dressing | Divide lettuce leaves and rinse in cold water. Drain well. Place in a large plastic bag in the refrigerator to crisp. Trim ends from spring onions. With the point of a sharp knife, slash either end about 5cm (2in) to give a fringed effect. Place in a bowl of icy water and chill well. As onions become chilled the ends will curl. Just before serving, tear lettuce roughly into a large salad bowl. Toss with spring onion curls. Garnish with watercress and croûtons and served accompanied with vinaigrette dressing. (See page 12.) |

# CHOCOLATE CREPES WITH PORT STRAWBERRIES

| | |
|---|---|
| 1 cup flour 3 tablespoons cocoa 1 cup milk ¼ cup water ⅛ teaspoon salt 2 tablespoons sugar 3 eggs 2 tablespoons clarified butter, melted extra butter for frying 1 litre (quart) prepared fruit | These may be served with any fresh fruit in season. Sift flour and cocoa into a bowl (or prepare in a food processor). Combine milk and water and stir into flour. Beat in remaining ingredients until smooth. Mixture should pour well. Grease a suitable crêpe pan with plenty of butter. Pour in 2–3 tablespoons of mixture and cook until just set. Flip over. Store cooked crêpes in a pile with waxed paper between. (To freeze; pile cooled crêpes, with a double layer of waxed paper between each crêpe, into an airtight container. Seal well. To serve; remove as many crêpes as required and thaw at room temperature about 15 minutes.) Serve 2 crêpes per person rolled around fresh fruit. If desired, warm crêpes (covered) in oven after duck has been removed and heat turned off. Fill with fruit after warming. The fruit can be sprinkled with castor sugar and soaked in liqueur e.g. strawberries soaked in port. Serve with whipped cream. Makes about 16 crêpes. |

# PASTA PROVIDES FUN EATING

## BRAISED FENNEL

## JUMBALAYA SAUCE AND PROSCIUTTO-TOMATO SAUCE WITH TWO PASTAS

## BASKET SALAD WITH BASIL MAYONNAISE

## LEMON LIQUEUR CREAM

A casual dinner for eight with lots of flavour. The fennel (finocchio) is blanched then braised and served with small new potatoes as a starter. Both pasta sauces should be served in heated casseroles or tureens and kept warm during the meal. Prepare the tomato sauce the day before and reheat when required. Allow guests to help themselves to the sauces and the pasta of their choice. Provide small bowls, forks and spoons for eating.

The salad is served with 1 or 2 dressings — the basil mayonnaise has a strong flavour.

Serve the lemon liqueur cream with a variety of accompaniments — toasted coconut, crisp almond biscuits, chocolate-dipped nuts and/or grapes.

# BRAISED FENNEL

3 fennel bulbs
salt
juice ½ lemon
16 tiny potato balls
2 tablespoons olive oil
2 tablespoons butter
freshly ground black pepper
sprigs of fennel for garnish

Blanch fennel in salted water with lemon juice for about 15 minutes. Remove. Cool. Cut into thin strips. Blanch potatoes until just tender.

Heat oil and butter in a large heavy saucepan over low heat. Add fennel and potatoes and sauté 10 minutes. Cover partially, stir occasionally. Serve on individual plates with potatoes, sprigs of fennel and garnished with lots of black pepper.

# JUMBALAYA SAUCE

500g (1lb) scallops
1 cup dry white wine
2 cloves garlic, crushed
2 tablespoons oil
1 cup cream
4 teaspoons cornflour
¼ cup water
1 teaspoon lemon juice
salt and pepper
250g (8oz) oysters
500g (1lb) shrimps (shelled)
2 spring onions or shallots, chopped
¼ cup finely chopped parsley

A mixture of shellfish in a wine and cream sauce. Other shellfish may be substituted according to taste.

Cut large scallops in half. Heat wine to boiling point, remove from heat. Stand scallops in the hot wine for 1 minute. Drain, reserving wine.

In a heavy pan heat oil, sauté garlic 1 minute, then add wine. Simmer 3 minutes. Add cream.

Mix cornflour and water to a smooth paste and stir into cream. Add lemon juice and seasonings. Add seafood to sauce and cook 2–3 minutes gently. Add onions and parsley. Serve in a heated tureen — keep warm during the dinner.

# PROSCIUTTO-TOMATO SAUCE

75g (3oz) prosciutto
1 tablespoon olive oil
1 large onion, diced
3x450g (15oz) cans Italian style tomatoes
¾ teaspoon dried basil
1½ teaspoons sugar
salt and pepper
¼ cup finely grated parmesan cheese
¼ cup finely chopped parsley

If prosciutto is unavailable use 125g (4oz) ham.

Dice prosciutto and sauté in a heavy pan in the oil with onion for 4 minutes. Add tomatoes and juices, basil and sugar. Mash tomatoes to break up. Simmer about 30 minutes until thick.

Season with salt and pepper. Serve in a tureen. Serve sprinkled with parmesan cheese and parsley.

# PASTA

Choose a total of about 1.5kg (3lb) of two different pastas. For example, spaghetti and green ribbon noodles. Fresh pasta is best but dried will suffice. Boil each pasta in separate saucepans using 4 litres (quarts) of boiling water to each 500g (1lb) of pasta. Add 1 teaspoon salt to the boiling water before slowly adding the pasta. Cook, uncovered, stirring occasionally, until just tender. Cooking time will depend on the type of pasta used. Drain well and mix with ½ cup melted butter. Keep warm in separate containers during the meal.

# BASKET SALAD

Fill a flat basket with crisp, prepared vegetables such as lettuce, spring onions, carrot and celery sticks, cucumber, and green peppers. Tomatoes and mushrooms may also be added. Select about 1kg (2lbs) vegetables for 8 people. Pass this Italian dressing with the basket, and/or serve a plain mayonnaise.

# BASIL MAYONNAISE

¾ cup packed fresh basil leaves
⅓ cup grated Parmesan cheese
3 tablespoons olive oil
1 egg
2 tablespoons lemon juice
1 clove garlic
½ cup melted butter
¾ cup salad oil

A version of 'pesto'.

Place basil leaves in a blender, and add cheese and oil. Blend until a thick purée is formed. Motor may need to be 'pulsed'. Remove from blender. Clean jar before proceeding.

Into the clean jar place the egg, lemon juice and garlic. Blend well. Add basil purée – mix. With motor running, drizzle in the melted butter and salad oil. Chill mixture. Serve in a bowl and use as a dip for the vegetables.

# LEMON LIQUEUR CREAM

1 cup lemon juice
4 teaspoons gelatine
½ cup sugar
⅛ teaspoon salt
4 large eggs, separated
¼ cup orange flavoured liqueur
¼ teaspoon cream of tartar
1 cup cream, whipped

Bring lemon juice to boiling point – allow to cool completely.

Combine juice and gelatine in a small saucepan. Add ¼ cup sugar, salt and the 4 egg yolks. Stir to blend. Cook over very low heat, stirring, until gelatine is dissolved.

Remove from heat and cool slightly. Add liqueur, stir well and refrigerate until mixture begins to thicken.

Add cream of tartar to egg whites and beat to the soft peak stage. Sprinkle in remaining sugar gradually, beating until shiny. Fold gelatine mixture into the egg whites.

Fold ⅔ of the whipped cream into the lemon mixture and spoon into 8 serving glasses. Refrigerate for several hours. Garnish with remaining cream.

# A SELECTION OF SATAYS

## LETTUCE ROLL

## SATAYS PRAWN
## PORK
## CHICKEN
## WITH THREE SAUCES
## GADO GADO
## PINEAPPLE SAMBAL
## RICE

## ALMOND JELLY

This menu is strongly influenced by South East Asian cuisine. Artistic licence has been taken though, to introduce some western ideas. It is an informal dinner and lots of fun.

Here, satays of three types are prepared for eight. A lettuce roll starter is easy to prepare — it incorporates some oriental ingredients but is more European in origin. The satays should be cooked over hot glowing coals if possible — a barbecue could be used — or use a good high temperature grill. Before threading meat onto bamboo skewers, soak sticks in water for

30 minutes to prevent them from burning. If barbecuing, guests can cook their own as required. If a grill is used, cook satays in batches.

A traditional Indonesian salad of cooked vegetables is an accompaniment plus a western version of a pineapple sambal. Boiled rice (see page 41) should also be served.

Almond jelly is a suitable ending with any fresh fruit in season. The jelly is prepared with agar agar which looks like powdered gelatine and also acts as a setting agent. It is prepared from seaweed.

# LETTUCE ROLLS

225g (8oz) ham, minced
150g (5oz) can crab meat
1 tablespoon oil
4 large mushrooms
4 spring onions
75g (3oz) can water chestnuts
125g (4oz) can bamboo shoots
2 teaspoons sesame seed oil
1 tablespoon soy sauce
1 tablespoon vinegar
8 lettuce leaves

Combine ham and crab meat. Heat oil over medium high heat and toss meat in this for 1 minute. Finely chop mushrooms and add to pan with diced spring onions, water chestnuts and bamboo shoots. Cook 1 minute. Combine remaining ingredients, add to pan, stir-fry 1 minute, then remove from heat. Filling can be served warm or at room temperature.

Trim lettuce leaves neatly. Place filling in centre. Guests fold ends and sides of lettuce over the filling to roll up the parcel. Makes 8 rolls.

# SATAY PRAWNS

500g (1lb) raw prawns
grated rind and juice of 1 large
lemon
½ cup coconut milk
1 canned chilli, diced
½ teaspoon dried shrimp paste
1 tablespoon soy sauce
1 teaspoon brown sugar
2 cloves garlic, crushed
1 teaspoon salt

Prawn Satay Sauce;

If raw prawns are unavailable then cooked can be substituted but there will be a flavour difference. If dried shrimp paste is unavailable then substitute anchovy paste.

Remove shells and veins from prawns. Combine all remaining ingredients in a bowl and marinate prawns for at least 15 minutes.

Thread 3–4 prawns onto bamboo skewers. Brush with oil and cook under a pre-heated grill on high, until lightly browned. Alternatively, the skewers may be cooked over glowing coals.

Combine marinade with ½ cup extra coconut milk and 1 tablespoon soy sauce. Slowly bring to the boil stirring. Simmer for 1 minute. Serve warm.

# SATAY PORK

1 large red onion
½ cup soy sauce
6 cloves garlic
⅛ teaspoon cumin
½ teaspoon ground turmeric
500g (1lb) lean pork

Pork Satay Sauce;
1 small red onion
2 cloves garlic, crushed
2 tablespoons oil
1¼ cups water
2 teaspoons each vinegar, sugar
1 tablespoon tomato sauce
1 tablespoon soy sauce
1 teaspoon crushed dried chilli
¼ cup crunchy peanut butter

Place the chopped onion, soy sauce, chopped garlic, cumin and turmeric into a food processor or blender and purée.

Cut pork into 1.5cm (½in) cubes. Marinate meat in the purée for at least 6 hours. Thread meat onto bamboo skewers about 6 pieces to a skewer.

Grill about 8 minutes, turning occasionally, until well browned.

Sauté diced onion and garlic in oil until golden. Add all other ingredients except peanut butter and bring to the boil. Simmer 3 minutes. Stir in peanut butter. Serve warm or at room temperature.

# SATAY CHICKEN

500g (1lb) boneless chicken
1 tablespoon coriander
1 teaspoon cumin
½ teaspoon fennel seed
1 large onion
2 cloves garlic
rind and juice 1 large lemon
1 tablespoon finely chopped
ginger root
1 teaspoon salt
1 teaspoon ground turmeric
2 teaspoons brown sugar
¼ cup oil

Cut chicken into approximately 1.5cm (½in) cubes.
Place coriander, cumin, and fennel into a dry pan and heat gently. Place in a blender or food processor with all other ingredients for the marinade, except oil. Purée.
Marinate chicken for at least 6 hours.
Thread meat onto bamboo skewers, about 6 pieces to a skewer. Brush with oil and grill until golden brown.

Chicken Satay Sauce;
1 cup plain yoghurt
grated rind 1 lemon
1 teaspoon cumin

Combine the ingredients. Use as a cold and refreshing sauce.

# GADO GADO

750g (1½lb) old potatoes
½ small cabbage
500g (1lb) long green beans
1 cup bean sprouts, blanched
1 large cucumber
1 onion
2 hard boiled eggs

Sauce;
5 fresh chillies
2 tablespoons oil
1 medium onion
1 cup coconut milk
⅓ cup crunchy peanut butter
2 teaspoons brown sugar
2 tablespoons lemon juice

Prepare salad vegetables well ahead. Boil potatoes until just tender — choose waxy potatoes if possible. Slice into 5mm (¼in) rounds. Shred and steam cabbage until bright green.
Cut beans into 4cm (1½in) lengths and steam until crisp tender. Blanch beansprouts in boiling water quickly then refresh in icy water.
Score cucumber and slice diagonally. Slice onion and hard boiled eggs. Just before serving arrange on a platter and pour over the sauce.
To make sauce, pound or chop chillies until fine. Heat oil in a saucepan and fry diced onion until soft. Add chillies and stir-fry for 5 minutes.
Stir in coconut milk slowly, then stir in all other ingredients and simmer 3 minutes or until sauce thickens. Cool.

# PINEAPPLE SAMBAL

2x454g (1lb) cans pineapple
chunks
1 small red onion, diced
1 small red pepper, diced
2 tablespoons vinegar
½ teaspoon salt

This side dish may also be prepared using fresh pineapple — add 2 teaspoons of sugar.
Drain pineapple and add onion, pepper, vinegar and salt. Stand 30 minutes before serving.

# ALMOND JELLY

3 cups water
4 teaspoons agar agar
1½ cups evaporated milk
½ cup sugar
½ teaspoon almond essence
1 litre (quart) fruit

Put water in a saucepan and sprinkle agar agar powder over it. Slowly bring to the boil, stirring, and simmer 5 minutes.
Add milk and sugar and stir gently until sugar is dissolved. Add flavouring.
Pour into a large rectangular dish and leave to set in refrigerator at least 1 hour.
To serve, cut jelly into diamond shapes and serve with fruit.

# CASSEROLE OF RABBIT

## ORANGE BLOSSOM CREAM AND FRUIT

## PROVENCE RABBIT WITH WHEATGERM

## CROUTON WITH STIR-FRY SPINACH SALAD

## CHOCOLATE FLUTES

Rabbit is mixed with bacon, herbs and spices in this dinner for eight.

It is one of the more economical meats and is readily available. Yet it is often considered too awkward to eat. Once the main bones are removed, that problem is solved. The wheatgerm in this country-style recipe provides an interesting coating,

and the bacon, tarragon vinegar and garlic a good taste combination.

For starters, fresh seasonal fruit is used. It should be arranged with imagination, and topped with a semi-sweet sauce.

Probably one of the most attractive methods of serving vegetables is the mixed stir-fry in large bread croûtons. The croûtons can be prepared well ahead and stored in an airtight container. The stir-fry is the only last minute cooking required in this menu.

For dessert, chocolate-fluted baskets are prepared by painting melted chocolate onto paper cases. They are filled with coconut covered ice cream and served with coffee liqueur. Both can be prepared several days in advance.

# ORANGE BLOSSOM CREAM AND FRUIT

Dressing;
½ cup fresh orange juice
1 tablespoon lemon juice
3 tablespoons sugar
2 egg yolks
salt and pepper
½ cup cream, whipped

1 litre (quart) fresh fruit

Use fresh fruit in season, e.g. figs, melon balls, or diced babaco. Choose something different.

To make sauce; place orange and lemon juice plus sugar in the top part of a double boiler. Stir over high heat until mixture boils. Remove from heat.

Beat egg yolks well adding a little of the hot juice. Then beat yolk mixture into the juice in the saucepan. Cook over hot water until creamy, stirring slowly. Season. Chill.

Just before serving fold in the whipped cream.

Arrange fruit attractively on 8 individual serving plates. Place a spoonful of sauce onto fruit and serve.

# PROVENCE RABBIT WITH WHEATGERM

2–3 rabbits
½ cup wheatgerm
salt and pepper
125g (4oz) butter
2 tablespoons tarragon vinegar
8 rashers bacon
3 cloves garlic
2 large onions
2 large carrots
4 sticks celery
2 tablespoons raw sugar
1½ cups white wine

Cultivated or farmed rabbits are ideal for this recipe. If using wild rabbit allow at least 30 minutes extra cooking time.

With a sharp knife, cut rabbits lengthways down centre back. Divide each rabbit into 6 portions, legs, body and forequarter. Remove bones from rib cage and fold flap under shoulder. Remove thigh bone from legs. Remove back bone from centre body portion. Allow about 200g (7oz) prepared rabbit per person.

Coat each piece of rabbit with seasoned wheatgerm.

Melt butter in a frypan and sauté rabbit pieces a few at a time, until just golden. Place in a large shallow casserole.

Deglaze frypan with vinegar and pour over meat. Wipe pan clean. Finely chop bacon and fry until crisp. Remove bacon to casserole.

Add crushed garlic to pan and diced vegetables. Sauté until golden. Stir in sugar. Add all to casserole.

Rinse pan with wine, bringing to the boil. Pour over casserole.

Cover and bake 180°C (350°F) for 1¼ hours.

## HOW TO JOINT A RABBIT

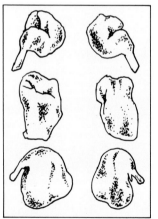

1. Slit rabbit lengthways down centre back.
2. Divide each rabbit into 6 portions, legs, body, and forequarter.
3. Remove bones from rib cage.
4. Remove bones from legs.
5. Remove bones from centre body portion.

# CROUTON WITH STIR-FRY

2 large loaves white bread
50g (2oz) butter

Stir-fry;
1 tablespoon oil
1 clove garlic, crushed
225g (8oz) button mushrooms
1 large onion, sliced
3 spring onions, sliced
200g (7oz) snow peas
8 canned baby corn ears
1½ cups bean sprouts, blanched
1 teaspoon sesame seed oil

A large, crisp bread croûton is filled with stir-fry vegetables. To blanch bean sprouts, drop quickly into boiling water for 30 seconds – refresh in icy water – pat dry.

To make croûtons, remove crusts from bread. Cut bread into 8cm (3in) cubes. With a sharp knife, cut 2cm (¾in) inside the cube, along the 4 sides. Cut to within 1cm (½in) of the base. Remove bread from centre with a teaspoon. Brush with melted butter. Bake 160°C (325°F) for about 12 minutes until golden and crisp.

Prepare vegetables for stir-fry and cook just before serving. Heat oil in a large heavy pan. Stir-fry garlic 1 minute. Add sliced mushrooms, onions, snow peas and baby corn and stir-fry 2 minutes. Add bean sprouts and sesame oil. Cover and cook 1 minute.

To serve, spoon mixture evenly into 8 croûton cases. Place on dinner plates alongside the rabbit.

# SPINACH SALAD

70g (2½oz) sliced almonds
1 tablespoon oil
¼ teaspoon dried basil
500g (1lb) spinach

Dressing;
2 tablespoons sugar
3 tablespoons cider vinegar
½ teaspoon salt
½ teaspoon dry mustard
½ cup oil
¼ teaspoon dried tarragon

4 sliced radishes

Sauté sliced almonds in 1 tablespoon oil and basil until lightly coloured. Drain on absorbent paper.

Wash spinach well in plenty of cold water. Remove any coarse stems. Drain. Crisp in a plastic bag in refrigerator. Just before serving tear leaves into a salad bowl.

To make dressing, dissolve sugar in the vinegar. Add salt, mustard, oil and tarragon and mix well. Toss salad in this dressing. Garnish with almonds and radishes.

# CHOCOLATE FLUTES

Chocolate flutes;
250g (9oz) cooking chocolate

Filling;
1 litre (1 quart) vanilla ice cream
1 cup flaked coconut
coffee liqueur

Chocolate cases are filled with rolled ice cream coated in toasted coconut.

To make flutes, break up chocolate and place in a pottery bowl over hot water. Stir until melted. Brush melted chocolate over the insides of 8 fluted baking cases. Allow to cool and harden. Repeat process until a thick layer of chocolate has been built up. Chill until solid. Carefully remove from baking cases.

Meanwhile, with an ice cream scoop, make 8 balls of ice cream. Place on a tray and freeze until solid. Lightly toast coconut in oven 180°C (350°F) for 10 minutes. Cool. Roll balls in this coconut and return to freezer.

Just before serving, place ice cream balls in chocolate flutes. Pass a small jug of coffee liqueur with the dessert.

# SOME LIKE IT HOT

## PICKLED FISH

## PORK ON FIRE
## CUMIN RICE
## MELON SALAD WITH FRUIT VINEGAR
## MIXED GREEN SALAD

## CHOCOLATE ZUCCHINI CAKE

Although this dinner for eight might appear to be highly seasoned there is a balance that will be appreciated. More or less chilli can be used according to taste.

Based on the characteristics of Latin American food, the pickled fish (or seviche) is a well-known marinated fish dish with chillies, and can be prepared up to 6 hours in advance.

The pork can be partially cooked the day before and finished just before serving. Choose attractive ramekins for serving. Taco chips make a suitable garnish and the rice absorbs some of the pork's fire.

Years of conquests by Spain, France and other European countries have influenced the cooking of Latin America — as is seen by the Mediterranean salad accompanying the main course.

Finally the ``pièce de résistance'' — a chocolate zucchini cake — a great keeper, rich, but complementary to the dinner.

# PICKLED FISH

850g (1¾lbs) lean white
boneless fish
1 cup fresh lime or lemon juice
2 tomatoes
1 medium onion, diced
2–3 chillies, canned or fresh
¼ cup olive oil
2 tablespoons white or cider
vinegar
1½ teaspoon oregano
½ teaspoon salt
white pepper
1 small red pepper
1 small green pepper
6 stuffed olives, sliced

Wipe fish, remove any dark pieces or skin. Cut into 2.5cm (1in) pieces. Place in a deep glass or ceramic bowl. Pour in lime juice and marinate in the refrigerator for at least 5 hours until fish takes on a 'cooked' appearance. Stir occasionally.

Just before serving, drain excess juice from fish. Add deseeded, peeled and chopped tomatoes, onion, chopped chillies, olive oil and vinegar combined, oregano, salt and pepper. Mix gently. Refrigerate until ready to serve.

Serve garnished with red and green peppers cut into strips.

# PORK ON FIRE

1 tablespoon each oil, butter
1.75kg (3½lb) lean,
boneless pork
2 cups chicken stock
1 tablespoon oil, extra
1 large onion, diced
3 cloves garlic, crushed
1 tablespoon paprika
450g (15oz) can tomatoes
4–6 chillies, canned
2 tablespoons tomato paste
1 teaspoon marjoram
½ teaspoon thyme
salt and pepper to taste

Add chillies according to taste!

Cut pork into 2.5cm (1in) pieces. Heat oil and butter in a heavy saucepan and brown pork. Remove any excess fat. Add stock, cover and simmer for 45 minutes. Lift out meat with a slotted spoon. Strain and reserve juices.

In a clean pan, heat 1 tablespoon oil. Add onions and garlic and cook until transparent. Add paprika, chopped tomatoes and chillies, and all other ingredients. Add enough juice to give a suitable amount of liquid. The mixture should be fairly dry. Simmer 15 minutes. This dish may be prepared to this point and continued just before serving.

Return meat to pan and cook uncovered 10–15 minutes. Serve immediately.

# CUMIN RICE

3 tablespoons olive oil
1 large green pepper, diced
1 large onion, diced
1 clove garlic, chopped
3 cups long grain rice
1½ teaspoons ground cumin
1 tablespoon chicken stock
powder
5 cups boiling water

This dish is pungent, not peppery, and complements the pork.

Heat oil in a large, heavy pan. Add pepper, onion, garlic and rice and cook until rice is lightly coloured. Add cumin and chicken stock dissolved in the water.

Cover and simmer on low heat for 30 minutes or until all liquid is absorbed and rice is tender.

# MELON SALAD WITH FRUIT VINEGAR

1 large cantaloupe melon
(or similar)
3 tablespoons sweet fruit vinegar
shredded lettuce

Peel melon and remove seeds. Cut into small dice. Sprinkle melon with vinegar (eg raspberry vinegar) and arrange on a bed of lettuce or in a suitable bowl.

# MIXED GREEN SALAD

1 large lettuce
2 onions
2 green peppers
4 tomatoes
3 hard boiled eggs
1 medium cucumber
8 black olives

Dressing:
¼ cup olive oil
¼ cup tarragon vinegar
½ teaspoon salt
freshly ground black pepper
1 clove garlic, crushed
2 tablespoons finely chopped
parsley

Wash lettuce, drain and crisp in refrigerator in a plastic bag. Slice onions finely and crisp in a bowl of icy water.

Just before serving, tear lettuce into small pieces and place in a salad bowl, adding sliced green peppers, tomatoes, and eggs. Peel and remove seeds from cucumber and cut into chunks. Add to salad with onion rings and sliced olives.

To make dressing, combine all ingredients in a blender and mix until well combined. At serving time toss salad in the dressing.

# CHOCOLATE ZUCCHINI CAKE

4 medium, firm zucchini
¾ cup chopped nuts
2 cups flour
1 teaspoon baking powder
¾ teaspoon each baking soda,
cinnamon, salt
¼ teaspoon nutmeg
150g (5oz) cooking chocolate
1½ cups sugar
3 eggs
½ cup plus 2 tablespoons oil
1 teaspoon vanilla
¾ cup milk
1 tablespoon lemon juice

Glaze:
100g (3½oz) cooking chocolate
50g (2oz) butter
¼ teaspoon oil
1 teaspoon golden syrup

Shred zucchini and squeeze out any excess moisture. Add nuts. Sift dry ingredients.

Melt chocolate in a double boiler over hot (not boiling) water. Beat sugar, eggs and oil until light, stir in vanilla. Alternately stir in the dry ingredients and milk. Add zucchini and nuts and mix well.

Pour into a lightly greased 20cm (8in) cake pan. Bake 50–60 minutes at 180°C (350°F). When cool the cake may be glazed.

Melt all ingredients in double boiler over hot water. Cool.

Spread over cake, allow to set in a cool place. May be decorated with almonds if desired.

# FLOWER FOOD

## MARIA'S CAPONATA

## WESTEND CHICKEN
## POTATO BASKET WITH CHRYSANTHEMUM SALAD
## CARROT PUDDING

## CAKE OF ROSES

The use of flowers in cooking prospered during ancient times. Romans incorporated flowers in their recipes as did the Mexican Aztecs. Today only a few countries use flowers in any great quantity as a food or flavouring although they are often now used as garnishes.

This unusual menu uses buds of flowers (capers) in the starter. Capers are grown mainly around the Mediterranean and influence the cooking of that area. The main course attracts a garnish of chrysanthemum petals and poppy seeds. Chrysanthemum leaves are often used in Japanese cooking (see page 15).

The dessert can be prepared 24 hours in advance and garnished at the last minute. Rose flavours the cake and flowers are used as a decoration.

Roses originated in Persia and this country was exporting rose water to China as far back as at the time of Christ. The flavour is still popular in desserts. Petals can also be used in preserves, liqueurs and wines. The rose symbolises love.

# Maria's Caponata

2 medium eggplants
6 tablespoons olive oil
2 cloves garlic, crushed
1 large onion, diced
2 stalks celery, diced
½ cup tomato puree
4 tablespoons capers
16 stuffed green olives, halved
¼ cup wine vinegar
2 tablespoons sugar
salt
freshly ground black pepper

Prepare this tasty, rich, cooked salad a day ahead.
Peel eggplants and cut into cubes.
Heat 4 tablespoons oil and sauté eggplant until coloured. Remove. Add remaining oil to pan. Sauté garlic, onion and celery until golden.
Add purée and simmer 2 minutes. Return eggplant to pan and add capers and olives. Heat vinegar and sugar and pour over the mixture. Season, cover and simmer 15 minutes, stirring occasionally. Cool, refrigerate.
Serve at room temperature with lemon wedges and toast.

# Westend Chicken

8 chicken legs
salt
3 cups fresh breadcrumbs
4 rashers ham, diced
4 spring onions, diced
1 teaspoon dried oregano
2 small eggs, lightly beaten
freshly ground black pepper
2 tablespoons oil
2 tablespoons butter
¾ cup chicken stock
¾ cup dry white wine
2 tablespoons tomato paste
24 asparagus tips, blanched
3 tablespoons poppy seeds

Allow 1 large chicken leg per person.
Remove bone and tendons from chicken legs with the help of a thin, sharp knife. Sprinkle chicken with salt.
Combine breadcrumbs, ham, onion, herbs, eggs and a few grindings of black pepper. Spoon stuffing into the chicken and shape to resemble chicken 'with bones'. Secure with toothpicks and string or cotton if need be.
Melt oil and butter in a heavy casserole and sauté chicken, a little at a time, until coloured on all sides. Add stock and wine and simmer, covered for 40 minutes, or bake in oven 180°C (350°F) for 45 minutes.
Carefully remove chicken to a warm platter — keep warm. Boil pan juices rapidly, stirring in tomato paste. Reduce liquid to half.
Place chicken portions (minus toothpicks) on serving plates. Spoon over the juice and garnish with asparagus and poppy seeds.

# Potato Basket with Chrysanthemum Salad

1.5kg (3lb) old potatoes
cornflour
oil for deep frying

Salad;
3 bunches watercress
3 pears
225g (8oz) green grapes
chrysanthemum petals
vinaigrette dressing (pg 12)

To make potato baskets (1 per person) peel and slice potatoes into julienne strips. Stand in cold water to which a tablespoon lemon juice or white vinegar has been added. Remove enough potato for 1 basket and pat dry thoroughly.
Toss potato in 1 teaspoon cornflour. Place in the bottom half of a potato nest basket (or substitute 2 wire sieves, 1 slightly larger than the other.) Fit second basket over the potatoes, pressing down firmly. Trim excess potato from base.
Deep fry in hot oil until golden. Remove from oil, remove top basket and gently prise the potato from base. Drain on absorbent paper. Keep in an airtight container until ready for service. Makes 8 baskets in all.
To make salad, wash and drain watercress and break into suitable serving pieces. (Spinach could be used as a substitute.) Peel and slice pears, sprinkling with lemon juice to retain colour if necessary. Halve grapes.
Just before serving, place watercress in each of the potato baskets and garnish with pears and grapes. Sprinkle with the petals of 2 unsprayed chrysanthemums, rinsed and patted dry. Place baskets on serving plates or accompanying side plates. Pass a vinaigrette dressing separately.

# HOW TO MAKE A POTATO BASKET

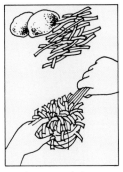

1. Julienne peeled potatoes and toss in cornflour. Cover bottom of a potato nest basket.

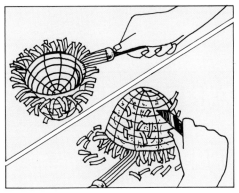

2. Fit 2nd basket over potatoes, trim excess.

3. Deep fry in hot oil until golden.

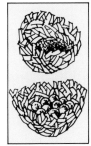

4. Remove top basket and gently prize basket from base. Drain on absorbent paper.

# CARROT PUDDING

6 large carrots, sliced
1 small onion, finely chopped
½ small green pepper
1 tablespoon oil
1 tablespoon flour
¼ teaspoon sugar
½ teaspoon salt
1 cup milk

Cook carrots in water until tender. Drain and mash well.

Sauté onion and finely diced green pepper in oil until onion is transparent. Stir in flour and seasonings. Cook 1 minute.

Whisk in milk. Cook until thickened, stirring. Add carrots.

Pour into a lightly greased 1.5 litre (3 pint) casserole. Bake 180°C (350°F) for 30 minutes.

# CAKE OF ROSES

Cake;
4 large eggs
¾ cup castor sugar
1¼ cups self-raising flour
1 teaspoon butter
3 tablespoons hot water

Beat eggs until light and thick. Gradually beat in sugar and continue beating until sugar is completely dissolved, about 10 minutes.

Sift flour several times. Melt butter in hot water.

Sift flour into egg mixture and fold in with water.

Pour into a 20cm (8in) cake pan which has been lightly greased and shaken with flour. Choose a tin with an interesting shape.

Bake 180°C (350°F) for about 25 minutes until cake is just starting to pull away from the sides. Turn cake onto a cake cooler.

Rose Filling;
750g (1½lb) cottage cheese
⅓ cup sugar
½ cup cream
3 tablespoons rose water or
1 teaspoon rose essence
2 tablespoons chocolate chips
½ cup chopped toasted almonds
½ cup candied citrus peel
⅓ cup chopped glace cherries
¼ cup white rum

Beat cheese, sugar, cream and rosewater until smooth. Add chocolate, nuts, fruit and chill. Slice cake through the centre into 2 layers.

Several hours before needed, place one layer on a serving plate and spread filling over the top. Place remaining cake on top and sprinkle with rum. Refrigerate until just before serving.

Topping;
icing sugar
crystallised flowers

Dust top of cake with icing sugar and garnish with flowers.

To make flowers, choose perfect, clean blooms. Brush each petal with lightly beaten egg white. Dip petals in castor sugar or icing sugar and place them on a plate which has been well sprinkled with the sugar. Sift a little more sugar over the flowers and leave to dry out in a warm place, 3–6 hours. (Use flowers within a few days.)

## PREPARE AHEAD

### CHILLI CHEESE

### ROASTED PORK IN ORANGE SAUCE
### POTATO VARIATION
### ASPARAGUS SESAME

### SWEETMEATS;
### CHOCOLATE PINKS
### FRUIT MARYLAND
### DIET DELIGHTS

Preparation for a dinner party can often be assisted by the home freezer, or at least dishes which can be prepared well in advance and refrigerated. This dinner for ten makes full use of the freezer.

The pork, potatoes and salad dishes can be frozen for up to 3 months ahead — if need be! (Seasonal fresh vegetables may be steamed and served as an accompaniment also.) The starter is a peppery cheese and it keeps well in the refrigerator. The dessert is a selection of sweetmeats which can be served with fresh fruit and coffee. The theme is simplicity, a major achievement for a large dinner party.

# CHILLI CHEESE

275g (10oz) cream cheese
275g (10oz) cheddar cheese, finely grated
1 clove garlic, crushed
2 large chillies
1 cup finely chopped walnuts
2 tablespoons chilli seasoning

Cream cheese together until smooth, add garlic, finely chopped chillies, and half the nuts. Shape into 2 rolls each about 4cm (1¾in) across.

Roll in combined chilli powder and nuts. Wrap each log in plastic film and chill. Keep for at least 3 days before using.

To serve, slice each log into 2cm (¾in) rounds and place on 10 individual serving plates with crisp celery and pita bread.

# ROASTED PORK IN ORANGE SAUCE

2kg (4lb) rolled boneless pork
salt and pepper
1 tablespoon oil
2 onions, thinly sliced
1½ cups orange juice
3 tablespoons vinegar
3 tablespoons red currant jelly

Garnish;
20 slices orange or segments of orange

Choose a boned and rolled loin or leg of pork. Remove rind and with the tip of a sharp knife score the skin finely – this may be frozen and roasted when required. To make crackling, rub the skin with oil and salt and cook 15 minutes at 230°C (450°F) then reduce heat to moderate for a further 10 minutes or until cooked. Keep in warming drawer while reheating main pork dish.

All excess fat should be removed. Rub meat with salt and pepper. Heat oil in a pan and lightly brown the meat. Place in a roasting pan with onions. Roast at 180°C (350°F) for 30 minutes. Combine remaining ingredients and pour over pork. Continue cooking for another 1 hour or until internal temperature is 75°C (170°F). Baste occasionally, turn once during cooking.

Cool quickly before freezing. Strain and cool juices, removing any fat. Meat may be frozen in the piece or sliced first. Cut into 5mm (¼in) pieces. Place in an airtight container. Brush with the strained juices. Cover tightly with plastic film, pressing film snugly onto the pork. Protect with an airtight cover. If freezing pork in the whole piece, wrap well in plastic, then in foil. Juices may be frozen separately.

To serve, remove from freezer about 12 hours before required and allow to thaw in refrigerator. Add a little extra fresh orange juice to sauce if required – reduce (boil) sauce until syrupy. Spoon over sliced meat in baking dish and reheat, lightly covered, in a moderate oven, 10–15 minutes. Place onto serving plates and garnish with warmed orange slices or segments. (If required, serve steamed seasonal vegetables as an accompaniment.)

# POTATO VARIATION

1kg (2¼lb) potatoes
1 egg
salt and pepper
1 beaten egg, extra
2 tablespoons water
flour
toasted breadcrumbs

Boil peeled potatoes until soft. Drain well, returning to element briefly to completely dry out the potato. Mash well, adding egg, and salt and pepper to taste.

Form into a cylinder and roll in flour. Cut into 10 even sized pieces. Brush with egg which has been lightly beaten with water. Roll in toasted breadcrumbs. Place on a baking tray.

Freeze until solid. Pack into a suitable airtight container and replace in freezer until required.

To serve, heat 2 tablespoons each oil and butter in a large frying pan. Place frozen potato into pan and cook about 5 minutes each side until golden and heated through.

# ASPARAGUS SESAME

1 kg (2 lb) trimmed asparagus

Dressing:
2 tablespoons soy sauce
2 teaspoons sugar
1 tablespoon sesame seed oil

Choose young, fresh asparagus for freezing or prepare this salad up to 4 hours before required. Thick ends should be removed from the stalks.

Bring a large saucepan of water to a rolling boil. Place half the asparagus in the pan and bring back to the boil for 1 minute. Chill asparagus in iced water for 3 minutes then pat dry. Repeat with remaining asparagus.

Place in a heavy plastic bag and seal top. Freeze, moving vegetables occasionally to prevent stalks from sticking together.

Two hours before required, remove from freezer and thaw in refrigerator. Toss with combined dressing ingredients and serve. If asparagus is unavailable, then small broccoli flowers could be used in the same way.

# CHOCOLATE PINKS

150g (5oz) white chocolate
1 cup sponge cake crumbs
2 tablespoons sherry
¼ cup ground almonds
¼ cup glacé cherries
1 tablespoon finely chopped crystallised ginger
few drops red food colouring
cherry slivers

Break up chocolate and melt over hot water. With a pastry brush, coat the insides of small paper patty cases. Allow to set in refrigerator then brush with more chocolate. Refrigerate overnight.

Combine cake crumbs, sherry, almonds, cherries, ginger and colouring. Roll into small balls and fit into chocolate cases. Freeze at this point if necessary, otherwise candies will keep for a few days in an airtight container in refrigerator.

To serve, remove paper cases, top with slivers of cherry and glaze with red jelly if desired. Makes about 15.

# FRUIT MARYLAND

125g (4oz) figs
225g (8oz) apricots
225g (8oz) seeded raisins
225g (8oz) walnuts
125g (4oz) candied lemon peel

Mince all ingredients coarsely. Add 1–2 tablespoons lemon juice if too dry. Roll into balls or a log about 2.5cm (1in) in diameter. Roll in icing sugar. Wrap in plastic film or place in a suitable container. Keeps very well in refrigerator. Makes about 30 balls.

# DIET DELIGHTS

¼ cup golden syrup
1 tablespoon boiling water
½ cup peanut butter
¾ cup skim milk powder
¾ cup sifted icing sugar
200g (7oz) chocolate
1 teaspoon vegetable shortening

Combine syrup and water until smooth. Mix well with peanut butter, milk powder and icing sugar. Roll into 2cm (¾in) balls. Refrigerate until firm.

Break up chocolate and melt with vegetable shortening in a china bowl over hot water (or in microwave for 2 minutes). With two forks rotate peanut balls in chocolate to coat. Place on a chilled tray which has been covered with foil. Refrigerate to set – these may have to be chilled as they are being prepared. Once set, chocolates may be refrigerated or deep frozen for up to 3 months. Makes about 25 chocolates.

# IT'S GAME FOR DINNER

## SEAFOOD CACCIATORE

## VENISON UNDER A PINE TREE

## PARSLEY POTATOES

## GARDEN CASSEROLE

## CARNIVAL TORTE

This dinner for ten is relatively easy to serve because most of it can be prepared in advance. The mixed seafood is coated in a spicy tomato sauce and grilled under low heat just before serving. If using sea (scallop) shells for serving they can be placed on a bed of rice or creamed potato to hold the shell firmly to a small serving plate.

The combination of minced venison and pork gives a mild flavour which appeals to many palates. The meat is cooked in individual servings and may be kept in the warming drawer if necessary, while the seafood is being grilled. Two or three extra servings could be cooked for those that require them. If muffin tins (or similar) are not available, then the meat may be cooked in a terrine or loaf pan and sliced for service — cook 180°C (350°F) for 1¼ hours. The garnish of thin fried noodles looks like a spray of pine needles. The accompanying layered garden casserole should be cooked in two casseroles, one per 5 people, which makes service easier, or in individual dishes.

The carnival torte uses fruit in season and imagination can be used for decoration.

# SEAFOOD CACCIATORE

1 kg (2 lb) mixed seafood
¼ cup lemon juice
2 tablespoons butter
2 cups tomato purée
2 cloves garlic, crushed
1 teaspoon salt
¼ teaspoon chilli powder
4 black peppercorns
1 onion, finely chopped
1 large green pepper, diced
2 cups sliced baby mushrooms
2 cups fresh breadcrumbs
¼ cup melted butter

Use a selection of seafood – lean white fish, scallops, baby mussels, shrimps etc.

Cut seafood into bite-sized pieces. Place on a buttered enamel plate and sprinkle with lemon juice. Dot with butter. Cover and cook over hot water. Cool and refrigerate until ready to use.

To make sauce, place purée, garlic, salt, chilli, peppercorns, onion, green pepper and mushrooms into a saucepan and simmer for 10 minutes. Remove peppercorns. Cool. Refrigerate until ready to use.

To make topping, toss breadcrumbs in butter and toast in hot oven until crisp and golden.

About 30 minutes before serving, reheat sauce in a heavy pan. Bring seafood to room temperature and reheat in sauce keeping similar fish together. Place a selection of seafood in 10 individual serving dishes (sea shells are suitable). Top with sauce and breadcrumbs. Place under a preheated grill on medium heat for 8–10 minutes, until heated through.

# VENISON UNDER A PINE TREE

1.25 kg (2½ lb) lean venison
500 g (1 lb) lean pork
2 eggs
¼ cup chopped parsley
¼ teaspoon white pepper
½ teaspoon sage
4 tablespoons tomato or fruit sauce
1 tablespoon sugar
2 cups fresh breadcrumbs

500 g (1 lb) peas

Brown sauce;
1 tablespoon oil
1 carrot, diced
1 onion, diced
2 tablespoons flour
2½ cups good brown stock
1 tablespoon tomato paste
bouquet garni

Trim any excess fat from meat. Mince finely twice. Mix well with all other ingredients. Lightly oil 10–12 deep muffin tins or ramekins. Spoon meat mixture into tins, pressing in firmly.

Bake 15 minutes at 180°C (350°F), remove foil and bake for a further 5 minutes. Turn onto serving plates and surround with hot green peas. Brush with brown sauce and pass a jug separately.

Heat oil in a small saucepan and sauté vegetables until lightly coloured. Stir in flour and cook until brown. Remove from heat and add half the stock, tomato paste and herbs. Stir well and bring to the boil. Simmer 15 minutes. Add remaining stock, strain and reheat gently.

# PINE TREE NOODLE GARNISH

Batter;
1 egg
1 tablespoon water
2 tablespoons cornflour
2 tablespoons flour
½ teaspoon each salt, sugar

50 g (2 oz) very thin round noodles
oil for deep frying

To make batter, beat egg well with water. Whisk in flours and seasonings until very smooth. Break noodles into 8 cm (3 in) pieces. Holding a little bunch firmly (about 25 short noodles), dip about 5 mm (¼ in) of one end into the batter. Next hold this end in hot oil for 5 seconds – this will fuse the ends together. Drop the noodles into the oil to brown – the unfused ends will fan out like pine needles. Remove as soon as they are golden. Prepare 10 sprays of 'needles'. Use as a garnish for the venison. Make a day in advance and keep in an airtight container.

# PARSLEY POTATOES

1.5kg (3lbs) potatoes
50g (2oz) butter
½ cup finely chopped parsley
freshly ground black pepper

Use small new potatoes or make balls of potato out of old ones. Use an extra 500g for this.

Boil peeled potatoes in plenty of boiling salted water until just tender, 15–20 minutes. Drain. Add melted butter and toss potatoes to coat. Sprinkle in parsley and pepper as desired.

# GARDEN CASSEROLE

1kg (2lb) carrots or pumpkin
1kg (2lb) parsnips
1kg (2lb) spinach
1 cup chopped parsley
5 small eggs
½ teaspoon nutmeg,
white pepper

Puréed vegetables are layered in a casserole and baked. May be prepared a few hours in advance then cooked when required.

Peel vegetables and steam each type separately until just tender. Remove thick stalk from spinach and steam with the parsley. Drain and purée each type separately. Season carrots with nutmeg and parsnips with pepper. Beat two eggs and add to carrot mix. Add another two to the parsnip. Add final beaten egg to spinach and parsley purée.

Grease two 1 litre (1 quart) casseroles. Divide purées between the two, placing spinach at base, then a layer of parsnip, then carrot (or pumpkin). Place casseroles in a baking pan low in the oven. Add enough water in the pan to come half way up the sides. Bake 35 minutes or until set, at 180°C (350°F). Garnish. (May also be prepared in individual casseroles.)

# CARNIVAL TORTE

Cake;
3 eggs
½ cup castor sugar
¾ cup self raising flour
1 teaspoon butter
2 tablespoons hot water

Two tortes should be prepared for 10 people.

Beat eggs until light and thick. Gradually beat in the sugar and continue beating until sugar is completely dissolved. Sift flour several times.

Melt butter in hot water. Sift flour into egg mixture and fold in with water.

Pour into a greased and lightly floured deep 20cm (8in) cake pan. Bake 180°C (350°F) for 20–25 minutes until cake is just starting to pull away from the sides of the tin. Turn out onto a cake cooler.

When cold, split into 3 layers horizontally.

Filling;
1 cup cream, whipped
3 tablespoons finely chopped toasted hazelnuts

Reserve ½ whipped cream for the outside of the cake. Fold hazelnuts into remaining cream. Place the base of the cake on a cake stand and spread with half of the hazelnut cream. Top with another layer of cake and spread with remaining hazelnut cream. Place last layer of cake on top. Refrigerate for at least 30 minutes.

Topping;
1 tablespoon gelatine
1 cup fruit juice
fresh fruit e.g.
red and golden tamarillos,
raspberries and strawberries,
or red and black currants

Soften gelatine in a little of the fruit juice. Dissolve in remaining juice over hot water. Allow to stand in the refrigerator until of egg-white consistency. Brush a layer of jelly over the top of the cake.

Peel and slice fruit. Place a layer of fruit attractively on top of the cake. Brush jelly carefully over the fruit. Allow to set in refrigerator. Then brush with more jelly. Allow to set.

Sides;
200g (7oz) cooking chocolate

Melt chopped chocolate in a china or glass bowl over hot water. (Do not overheat as chocolate will lose its shine.) Pour melted chocolate into a large tray lined with greaseproof paper and spread out evenly to 5mm (¼in) thickness. Allow to harden.

Peel off paper and using a sharp knife cut chocolate into oblongs about 2.5cm (1in) wide and the depth of the cake.

Spread a thin layer of the reserved whipped cream around the outside of the cake. Stand strips of chocolate around the outside edge. Pipe whipped cream around outside edge. Serves 5–6.

## HAIL AVOCADO, TURKEY AND BLUEBERRIES

### AVOCADO MOUSSE

### BONELESS TURKEY WITH THREE STUFFINGS

### CRISPY ROASTED YAMS

### CELERY SALAD WITH WALNUT OIL DRESSING

### BLUEBERRY HEARTS

Mastering the art of boning poultry is probably best practised on a chicken. Follow steps carefully — if any holes are made in the skin by accident, just sew up with cotton. This stuffed turkey recipe is a talking point and is also easily and quickly carved for ten people. The entire menu has an American slant.

Serve the turkey garnished with lychees stuffed with crystallised ginger, rolled in bacon and gently grilled — prepare ahead and serve at room temperature.

The salad of celery and apples has a definite walnut flavour with the dressing. Other salads may be incorporated into the menu if hearty appetites are expected, or brioche or croissants may be served.

The blueberry hearts are fun — fresh, frozen or canned fruit may be served with the hearts of a soft, waffle-like mixture.

# Avocado Mousse

4 medium avocados
1 small onion, grated
2 tablespoons lemon juice
¼ teaspoon white pepper
few drops Worcestershire sauce
2 tablespoons powdered gelatine
¼ cup cold water
½ cup boiling water
1 cup cream, whipped
¼ cup mayonnaise

Mash avocado flesh until smooth, with onion, lemon juice and seasonings. Soften gelatine in cold water. Add boiling water and dissolve gelatine. Cool until it reaches an egg-white consistency. Fold in whipped cream, mayonnaise and avocado. Pour into ten individual moulds (e.g. patty pans) and refrigerate to set.

To serve, unmould onto serving plates and garnish with prawns, carrot curls or other suitable garnish.

# Boneless Turkey with Three Stuffings

3.5kg (7–8lb) turkey
500g (1lb) fresh spinach
salt and pepper
2 cups fresh breadcrumbs
1 egg
1 small onion, diced
2 tablespoons butter
1 teaspoon mixed herbs
1½ cups minced ham
1 cup white wine

Garnish;
(see introduction)

Wine sauce

Remove bones from turkey as in diagram but leave wing and leg bones in so bird can be reshaped more easily.

Wash spinach, discard any thick stalks and chop coarsely. Place in a large saucepan and cook until limp. Season with salt and pepper. Squeeze to remove excess moisture. Chop.

Combine breadcrumbs with beaten egg, onion sautéed in butter and mixed herbs.

Place boned-out turkey skin side down, on a board. Place spinach stuffing down one third of the cavity. Spoon bread stuffing down the next third, then finally the ham. Fold the skin and flesh neatly back around the stuffing, bringing the wing and leg ends back against the body.

Sew up the back with double cotton. Tie with string to keep a good shape.

Place in a roasting bag – use according to manufacturer's instructions. Roast for 25 minutes per 500g (1lb) at 180°C (350°F). Place on a warmed serving platter and stand in warming drawer while making the wine sauce.

Place juices in a saucepan removing any excess fat by lightly placing a thick slice of bread on top of the liquid to absorb the fat. Bring juices to a rolling boil and add 1 cup good white wine. Continue boiling until reduced by about one third. Thicken with 2 tablespoons cornflour mashed with 2 tablespoons butter – add a little at a time.

## How to Bone a Turkey

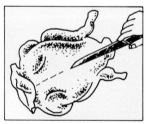

1. Place turkey on breast and slit skin down backbone cutting from neck to tail.

2. Scrape along one side of spine to separate meat from bones.

3. Continue around ribs on either side of bird to meet at breast bone. Lift out carcass.

4. Snip sinews at wing joints.

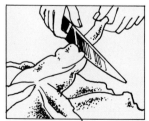

5. Scrape flesh along wing bone, turing wing inside. Bone tip may be left for shape.

6. Cut through leg joint, snip sinews and scrape flesh away from bone as for wings.

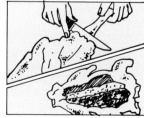

7. Lay bird flat on skin side, and place stuffings down length.

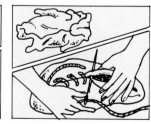

8. Fold skin and flesh neatly over stuffing and sew up with cotton. Shape well.

# CRISPY ROASTED YAMS

1.5kg (3lb) yams
½ cup flour
2 teaspoons salt
2 tablespoons oil
50g (2oz) butter

Use yams or sweet potatoes.

Wash and scrub vegetables. Peel and cut into serving sized pieces if necessary. Place flour and salt in a plastic bag and shake vegetables in this to coat well. Heat oil and butter in a large frypan, preferably one with a non-stick coating. An electric frypan is suitable.

Add vegetables, partially cover and cook 15 minutes. Turn vegetables and continue cooking until tender, basting occasionally. Remove cover at end and crisp the vegetables.

# CELERY SALAD WITH WALNUT OIL DRESSING

8 large stalks celery
4 red-skinned apples
¼ cup finely chopped parsley
½ cup lemon juice
⅓ cup walnut oil
salt and pepper
onion rings

Choose fresh, crisp, green stalks of celery. Remove any stringy pieces and dice. Core apples and cut into a similar size. Toss with parsley and combined lemon juice and walnut oil. Season with salt and pepper. Just before serving, garnish with onion rings which have been soaked in icy water to crisp. Serve in a tall glass bowl.

# BLUEBERRY HEARTS

1 cup flour
1 teaspoon baking powder
¼ teaspoon salt
1 egg
¼ cup sugar
½ cup milk
2 tablespoons oil
¼ cup extra milk


Topping;
maple syrup
blueberries
whipped cream and/or
plain yoghurt

Sift dry ingredients. Beat egg with sugar and pour in milk and oil. Combine with dry ingredients until smooth (in food processor if you wish).

Add extra milk if necessary to make a pouring batter.

Brush a heavy frypan with butter. Heat to about 190°C (375°F). Place a heart-shaped biscuit cutter on the pan and pour a little batter into the mould.

Cook until bubbles break on the topside of the hearts, remove mould and flip it over to cook other side. Remove to a cake cooler, and prepare another heart. (Cook 10.) These may be prepared ahead and frozen if required. Reheat in microwave oven 15 seconds per heart, or covered in a low temperature 160°C (325°F) conventional oven for about 5 minutes.

Serve hearts on individual dishes topped with fresh, frozen and thawed, or canned blueberries. Pass syrup, cream and yoghurt separately.

## SOMETHING COOL

### LEMON CHICKEN AND CRISPY NOODLES

### TROPICAL SALAD PLATE WITH GREEN DRESSING
### CHEESE COBB

### TRIPLE DIPPED STRAWBERRIES WITH COCONUT RUM ICE CREAM

The preparation for this summertime meal may take time, but there is little last minute panic. The lemon chicken is appealing in colour and taste. It is a hot stimulating start to a cold dinner and may be cooked ahead then reheated. The salad platter can use any seasonal vegetable or fruit but fresh, clean, bright ingredients are essential. Prepare and carefully store in covered bowls in refrigerator until ready to arrange on serving plates. Dishes can be organised an hour in advance and kept covered in a cool place.

Flowers for the ten guests make a lasting impression as do the strawberries which are dipped in 3 types of chocolate and served with a flavoursome ice. The berries should be prepared no more than 5 hours ahead of serving time as they may start to weep.

# LEMON CHICKEN AND CRISPY NOODLES

2kg (4lb) chicken wings
1 large lemon
1 teaspoon light soy sauce
1 cup water
1 tablespoon sugar
1 teaspoon sesame oil
1 tablespoon cornflour
2 tablespoons cold water
1 tablespoon oil
1 tablespoon finely grated root ginger
few drops lemon food colouring
5 spring onions

If desired, cut off wing tips at joint and discard or use in another dish. Peel lemon very thinly. Slice peel into thin strips. Squeeze lemon and measure about ⅓ cup lemon juice. Combine juice, rind, soy, water, sugar and sesame oil.

Mix cornflour to a smooth paste with the 2 tablespoons cold water.

Heat oil in a wok or large frypan and fry wings both sides until golden. Add ginger and fry 1 minute. Add lemon juice mixture, bring to the boil, cover and reduce heat until just simmering. Cook about 15 minutes until chicken is tender. Remove chicken to a warm platter.

Stir in cornflour and cook until thickened. Add a few drops of lemon food colouring to heighten the colour. Pour over chicken and serve garnished with spring onions. Serve on a large platter or in individual bowls. Finger bowls could be supplied, or wings can be served on a base of crispy noodles.

# CRISPY NOODLES

250g (9oz) transparent rice noodles
oil for deep frying

Break off enough noodles for 1 serving, arrange in a compact shape and deep fry in hot oil until puffed and crisp. Make ten servings. Keep in an airtight container if prepared ahead.

# TROPICAL SALAD PLATE WITH GREEN DRESSING

For each serving allow:
3 button mushrooms
¼ cup alfalfa sprouts
4 king prawns (cooked)
½ cup crab meat, or
4 steamed mussels
3 slices pastrami
3 wedges tomato or kiwifruit
¼ papaya (pawpaw), sliced
1 passionfruit, halved
4 lettuce leaves
3 slices ham or salami
2–3 green pepper fans

Green dressing:
1 cup sugar
1 teaspoon salt
1 teaspoon dry mustard
½ cup cider vinegar
1¼ cups salad oil
1 finely chopped spring onion
½ finely diced green pepper

Wash and prepare vegetables and fruit. Score mushrooms with a sharp knife. To make green pepper fans, cut a large green pepper in half lengthwise and carefully remove seeds and ribs. Cut each half in quarters. Make 4 even cuts in the broad end of each pepper almost to the other end. Soak in iced water for several minutes until the fan opens slightly.

Arrange ingredients on 10 plates in a similar way as shown in the photograph. If to be prepared ahead then cover loosely with plastic film.

Serve with the sweet and sour green dressing.

Combine sugar, salt and mustard in a small heavy saucepan. Stir in vinegar. Boil 1 minute. Cool. Place in a blender and with the motor running, slowly drizzle in oil. Stir in onion and green pepper. Chill.

# CHEESE COBB

2 round cobb loaves
225g (8oz) butter
1 clove garlic, crushed
¼ cup finely chopped parsley
1 cup finely grated cheddar
cheese

Parallel cut the loaves, every 2cm (¾in) almost through to the other side. Turn loaves and cut at right angles in a similar manner.

Blend butter until smooth and add seasonings. Spread evenly throughout the bread. Sprinkle each loaf with cheese. Bake in oven, 180°C (350°F), loosely covered with foil, for 10 minutes. Serve hot.

# TRIPLE DIPPED STRAWBERRIES WITH COCONUT RUM ICE CREAM

Ice cream;
1½ cups sugar
1 cup water
2 x 450g (16oz) cans coconut milk
½ cup white rum

30 strawberries with sepals
150g (5oz) white chocolate
150g (5oz) dairy milk chocolate
150g (5oz) dark chocolate

To make ice cream, boil sugar and water 1 minute, stirring gently to dissolve sugar. Cool.

Combine syrup with coconut milk and rum. Chill. Place in an ice cream maker for best results and churn until thick and ready to freeze. Otherwise, freeze until almost solid, beat well with an electric beater then freeze again until solid.

To prepare strawberries, melt chopped white chocolate in a small bowl over hot water (or in microwave about 1 minute). Holding the strawberry by the sepals, dip each one into the chocolate so that it coats ¾ of the strawberry. Allow to set in refrigerator. Then dip into melted but cooled, dairy milk chocolate, to nearly cover the white chocolate. Refrigerate to set. Finally dip the tips of each strawberry into the melted dark chocolate. Refrigerate.

Serve 3 strawberries per serving on individual plates with the ice cream.

## TWELVE SIT DOWN FOR DINNER

### CURRIED EGGPLANT SOUP

### ROLLED BEEF WITH SPINACH

### MUSHROOMS IN DARK SAUCE

### VEGETABLE TARTS

### CURRANT SURPRISE

### WALNUT AND MOCHA PIE

*Eggplant and curry powder make a chilling entrance to this dinner. The combination is tasty, and popular served very cold.*

The beef is an economical cut of skirt (flank) steak which is rolled around spinach and diced carrots. Prepare ahead, up to the point of cooking. Oven roasting takes approximately 1½ hours. Small tarts with vegetables are an unusual but easy accompaniment. The saucy mushrooms complement the beef.

A mixture of brown rice, coconut, and red or black currants is the salad.

The dessert can be prepared in a cake or baking pan. The pie base is crushed walnuts, not biscuit crumbs. The filling is a light combination of chocolate, whipped egg whites and cottage cheese. This can be prepared a day or two ahead.

# CURRIED EGGPLANT SOUP

50g (2oz) butter
2 medium onions, diced
2 tablespoons curry powder
1.5kg (3lb) eggplant
2 litres (quarts) chicken stock
1 cup cream
½ teaspoon salt
½ teaspoon pepper

In a large heavy saucepan, melt butter over medium heat and add onion. Sauté, stirring occasionally, until soft. Add curry powder and cook 2 minutes.

Add peeled and diced eggplant and chicken stock, and bring to the boil. Cover and simmer 45 minutes or until eggplant is soft. Transfer to a blender or food processor and purée until smooth.

Add cream and seasonings and chill for at least 4 hours. Garnish with finely chopped parsley. (This soup can also be lightly warmed.)

# ROLLED BEEF WITH SPINACH

4 skirt steaks (about 2kg or 4lb)
oil
freshly ground black pepper

Stuffing;
1kg spinach
1 large onion, finely diced
1 large carrot, finely diced
2 tablespoons butter
1½ cups fresh breadcrumbs
1 egg, beaten

Divide skirt steaks in half through the centre to make 8 steaks. Using the tip of a sharp knife, score skirt steaks on the smooth side, in a crisscross manner. Turn steaks scored side down.

Prepare stuffing; Wash spinach and remove any coarse stems. Chop. Place in a large saucepan and cook until wilted. Drain well, squeezing out excess moisture. Chop finely. Sauté onion and carrot in butter until onion is soft and add to spinach with breadcrumbs and enough egg to bind.

Place stuffing onto the meat and roll up from the long side, as for a sponge roll. Secure with skewers or tie every 3cm (1½in).

Brush with oil and sprinkle with black pepper. Place in a baking pan and roast, lightly covered, for 1½ hours at 180°C (350°F), turning once and removing cover during last 15 minutes.

To serve, place meat onto a serving dish and slice into 2.5cm (1in) pieces.

# MUSHROOMS IN DARK SAUCE

1kg (2lb) mushrooms, sliced
50g (2oz) butter
2 tablespoons flour
1¼ cups beef or vegetable stock
2 tablespoons soy sauce
½ teaspoon brown sugar

Sauté mushrooms in butter, in a large heavy saucepan. When soft, sprinkle in the flour. Remove from heat.

Gradually add stock, stirring. Reheat gently, stirring. Add soy sauce and sugar.

# VEGETABLE TARTS

Pastry recipe (see page 20)

1½ cups whole kernel corn
1½ cups peas
2 tablespoons butter

To make 24 tarts, roll out pastry to 5mm (¼in) thickness. Cut out 8cm (3in) rounds with the help of a biscuit cutter. Line patty pans with the pastry. Chill 30 minutes, then bake 190°C (375°F) for 10 minutes until golden.

When cool these may be stored in an airtight container until ready to fill. Pastry shells may be warmed in a warming drawer before serving.

Cook corn and peas separately. Drain and mix into each, a tablespoon of butter. Fill one half of the shells with corn and the other with peas.

# CURRANT SURPRISE

5 cups cold cooked brown rice
4 cups red (or black) currants
2 stalks celery, diced
1 cup desiccated coconut

Dressing;
2 tablespoons honey
¼ cup lemon juice
¾ cup oil
salt and pepper

Combine rice carefully with currants, celery and coconut. Mix dressing ingredients well. Just before serving, fold into salad.

Boiled brown rice;
1¾ cups raw brown rice
6 cups water
1 teaspoon salt

Rinse rice well under the cold water tap.
Place in a saucepan with the 6 cups of water and salt. Cover and cook over low heat about 45 minutes or until just tender and most of the liquid as been absorbed. Drain in a sieve. Cool before using in the above recipe.

# WALNUT AND MOCHA PIE

350g (12oz) walnuts
½ cup brown sugar
100g (3½oz) butter

Filling;
500g (1lb) cottage cheese
250g (9oz) dairy milk chocolate
1 tablespoon coffee flavoured liqueur
2 tablespoons gelatine
½ cup white sugar
4 eggs, separated
1 cup milk
2 tablespoons castor sugar

To make base, first lightly toast walnuts in oven. Chop finely – about 5mm (¼in) dice. Melt brown sugar and butter and stir into walnuts. Press into a 25cm (10in) square pan which has been very lightly greased with butter. Chill until firm.
Beat cottage cheese until smooth.
Melt chopped chocolate over hot water. Cool slightly, and add to cheese with liqueur.
Combine gelatine, white sugar, egg yolks and milk in the top part of a double boiler – beat well. Cook over hot water until thick, stirring. Cool. Beat into cottage cheese.
Whip egg whites until stiff. Gradually add castor sugar, beating until shiny. Fold into cheese mixture. Pour onto base and chill.
To serve cut into 12 squares. Pipe with whipped cream and garnish with fresh tangy fruit (e.g. orange segments, kiwifruit slices etc.).

## LIGHT COOKING

### YABLOCHNY

### EMERALD AND GINGER FISH
### CARROTS VERMOUTH
### SALAD SKEWER
### WITH LO-CAL DRESSING
### PUMPKIN CRESCENTS

### DAMIEN'S PEACH FREEZE

It is a pleasant combination of cinnamon, puréed apple and dry wine. Serve warm or chilled — refrigerate a day before using if serving chilled.

The fish is prepared in individual servings, seasoned with ginger and lemon and wrapped in blanched lettuce leaves. It can be prepared up to the cooking point, and refrigerated. It is then baked for 25 minutes prior to serving. The carrots have a faint vermouth glaze, the croissants (or crescents) are for those who do not mind adding about 545 kilojoules (130 calories) to their meal.

The dessert is a frozen purée of peaches mixed with (low-fat) yoghurt. Both the dessert and the crescents can be prepared weeks ahead and frozen.

This dinner menu has been prepared with a thought to the waistline. Yablochny is an apple soup based on a Russian recipe.

# YABLOCHNY

1.5kg (3lb) cooking apples
¾ cup boiling water
1 stick (quill) cinnamon
zest of 1 lemon
2 tablespoons dried breadcrumbs
3 tablespoons lemon juice
¼ cup lemon juice
1½ cups dry white wine

Peel, core and slice apples. Place in a heavy saucepan with water, cinnamon, zest and breadcrumbs. Simmer until soft. Remove cinnamon quill.

Purée until smooth. Chill thoroughly. When ready to serve, add sugar which has been dissolved in the lemon juice and the white wine. Add extra wine if mixture is too thick. Serve chilled or lightly warmed.

# EMERALD AND GINGER FISH

2kg (4lb) lean white fish
12 large lettuce leaves
lemon juice
sesame seed oil
4 tablespoons finely diced
ginger root
salt and pepper
12 small sprigs parsley
1 cup chicken stock

Halibut, monkfish, snapper, John Dory, cod, flounder are suitable types of fish to use in this recipe.

Divide fish into 12 suitable sized serving pieces.

Blanch lettuce leaves in boiling water, one at a time, until limp but bright green. Remove any coarse pieces from stem. Drain well. (Leaves should be large enough to roll around the fish — if using smaller leaves then overlap several to make cover large enough.)

Place each piece of fish in the middle of the lettuce leaves. Top each with a squeeze of lemon juice, 2 drops sesame seed oil, 1 teaspoon of ginger root, salt and pepper and a small sprig of parsley. Fold up lettuce to enclose the fish.

Place in a large baking pan with folded edges underneath the fish. Add enough chicken stock to just cover base of pan. Cover lightly with foil and bake 190°C (375°F) for about 25 minutes, until fish is just cooked. Serve onto dinner plates.

# CARROTS VERMOUTH

12 medium carrots
½ cup dry vermouth
3 tablespoons sugar
2 tablespoons white wine vinegar

Peel carrots and stamp into designs using a vegetable or biscuit cutter. Use offcuts for another meal. Bring carrots to the boil in a large saucepan with boiling water to nearly cover. Cook until just tender. Drain and chill in icy water for about 5 minutes. Drain and refrigerate until ready to serve.

Simmer vermouth, sugar and vinegar until syrupy. This may be refrigerated until ready to use.

To serve, allow both to come to room temperature first. Heat carrots in vermouth stirring to coat in glaze.

# SALAD SKEWER WITH LO-CAL DRESSING

½ zucchini
2–3 button mushrooms
¼ green and red pepper
2 cauliflowerettes
2 stalks blanched asparagus
1 sliced spring onion
1 baby corn
1 tomato
2 wedges cucumber

Lo-cal dressing:
1 tablespoon cornflour
1 teaspoon dry mustard
¼ teaspoon salt
¾ cup cider vinegar
¾ cup water
few drops artificial liquid
sweetener

A selection of seasonal vegetables (or fruits) may be chosen. Amounts given are for 1 serving.

Wash and prepare vegetables. Cut vegetables into mouthful size. Thread onto bamboo skewers allowing about 2 per person. Brush with a little dressing before serving on platters or on individual dinner plates.

Combine cornflour, mustard and salt in a saucepan. Mix well with the vinegar and water and bring to the boil over medium heat. Cool and add liquid sweetener to taste. Chill. Serves 12.

# PUMPKIN CRESCENTS

1 tablespoon dried yeast
2 tablespoons sugar
2 tablespoons warm water
3¾ cups flour
½ teaspoon salt
50g (2oz) butter
¼ cup warm milk
1 small egg, lightly beaten
225g (8oz) pumpkin (or
squash), cooked and puréed
2 tablespoons finely chopped
toasted nuts

Cook peeled pumpkin or similar until soft. Mash. Dry out over low heat if necessary – mixture should be like a thick apple pulp.

Dissolve yeast and 2 tablespoons of sugar in water and set aside. Place remaining ingredients in a large bowl. Rub in half the butter until mixture resembles breadcrumbs.

Stir in the yeast mixture, milk, egg and purée, and mix well, until shiny. Place in a well greased bowl, cover with plastic film and stand in a warm place until doubled in bulk, about 2 hours.

Punch dough down, knead for 3 minutes, divide dough in half and form both into circles about 1cm thick. Melt remaining butter and brush over dough. Sprinkle with nuts. With a sharp knife, cut circle into quarters then into eighths.

Starting at the wide end, roll up dough toward the points. Use a spatula and place rolls on greased oven trays. Curve ends around to form a half moon. Cover with greased plastic and leave to rise in a warm place until double in size.

Place in a hot oven 220°C (425°F). Bake 10 minutes or until lightly browned.

# DAMIEN'S PEACH FREEZE

4 cups sliced, peeled, cooked,
peaches
1 tablespoon vanilla
¾ teaspoon each ground
nutmeg, cinnamon
3 eggs, separated
⅛ teaspoon salt
¼ teaspoon cream of tartar
¼ cup castor sugar
1 litre plain yoghurt

Choose sweetened peaches – otherwise add ¼ cup liquid honey. Purée fruit. Place over medium heat until almost boiling. Remove from heat and add vanilla and spices.

Beat egg yolks until creamy then add a little of the hot purée – mix well. Stir into remaining purée.

Beat egg whites, salt and cream of tartar until stiff. Gradually add the sugar until a meringue consistency is formed.

Mix fruit into yoghurt until well combined. Fold this into egg whites. Refrigerate until well chilled.

Freeze preferably in an ice cream machine or freeze until almost solid. Beat well then refreeze. May be served with coconut flakes, toasted almonds or berries.

## FORK FOODS FOR TWELVE

### PISTACHIO AND SPICY BEAN DIPS WITH VEGETABLES

### TAMALE PIE
### LONG BEAN SALAD WITH HONEY DRESSING
### SUNRISE SALAD

### MT ORANGE SOUFFLE

A spicy dinner for which the grand 'finale' is a rich orange soufflé.

Pistachio nuts have a beautiful green kernel which can be roasted and salted like other nuts or used as flavourings and colour in desserts. They also make an attractive dip for vegetables.

The tamale pie is hot and spicy — choose the number of chillies with thought to the character of your guests. The dips and the meat may be prepared a day or two in advance.

Both salads complement the flavour and colour of the pie. Serve hot, crispy bread if required or a pot of panfried zucchini. Allow 1 per person — slice thinly into a heavy pot with 75g (3oz) melted butter — stir fry until just tender.

Although the egg yolks used in this dessert are numerous, the Mt Orange soufflé is a taste experience well worth trying.

# PISTACHIO DIP

1 large egg
2 tablespoons lemon juice
2 tablespoons white wine vinegar
½ teaspoon mustard
½ teaspoon salt
⅔ cup safflower oil
⅓ cup olive oil
1 clove garlic, crushed
1 spinach leaf, chopped
3 tablespoons chopped parsley
½ teaspoon dried tarragon
⅔ cup pistachio nuts

Serve both these dips with a selection of crisp vegetable dippers such as cauliflowerettes, capsicums (sweet peppers), cucumber and carrot sticks, button mushrooms, spring onions, celery, and radishes.

Place egg, lemon juice, vinegar, mustard and salt in a blender or food processor fitted with a steel blade. With motor running, slowly drizzle in the oils. Then add remaining ingredients, blending until sauce is flecked with green. Cover and refrigerate until ready for use.

# SPICY BEAN DIP

300g (10½oz) canned red kidney beans
2 cloves garlic, crushed
1 teaspoon Worcestershire sauce
dash Tabasco sauce
2 tablespoons cider vinegar
1 spring onion, finely chopped

Drain kidney beans reserving liquid. Place beans with all other ingredients into a blender or food processor. Blend until well combined (or mash with a fork). Add enough liquid from beans to make a dipping consistency. Refrigerate and serve chilled.

# TAMALE PIE

2 large onions, chopped
2 green peppers, diced
2 tablespoons oil
2kg (4lb) lean minced beef
2 cups tomato purée
3 cups whole kernel frozen corn
1 cup sliced stuffed olives
1 tablespoon ground cumin
2 tablespoons cocoa
1½ teaspoons allspice
4–6 teaspoons chilli powder
1 tablespoon Worcestershire sauce
1 teaspoon Tabasco sauce
3 tablespoons yellow cornmeal
salt and pepper

Topping:
2 cups flour
2 cups yellow cornmeal
⅓ cup sugar
4 teaspoons baking powder
100g (3½oz) butter, melted
1 cup milk
2 eggs, beaten
1 cup finely grated tasty cheddar
⅓ cup finely chopped chillies

In a large frypan, sauté onion and pepper in oil until soft. Add beef and cook until coloured. Add tomato purée, corn, olives, cumin, cocoa, allspice, chilli powder, Worcestershire, Tabasco, cornmeal, salt and pepper. Simmer, covered, stirring occasionally, for about 10 minutes. Place in 2 large casseroles or similar. This mixture may be kept overnight in the refrigerator.

To prepare topping, combine flour, cornmeal, sugar and baking powder with butter, milk, and egg until batter is just mixed. Stir in cheese and chillies. Drop by large spoonfuls around the edge of casserole.

Bake 200°C (400°F) for 10 minutes then at 180°C (350°F) for 30 minutes or until hot and cooked through.

# Long Bean Salad
# With Honey Dressing

1 kg (2 lb) long green beans

Dressing;
¼ cup white wine vinegar
¼ cup honey
1 teaspoon paprika
¾ cup safflower oil

String beans and cut into long strips (with a bean cutter). Bring a large saucepan of water to the boil. Boil beans 2 minutes or until crisp-tender. Refresh in icy water 5 minutes. Drain well and pat dry. Place on a serving plate. Cover and chill.

To make dressing, blend vinegar, honey and paprika together until smooth. With motor running in blender, slowly drizzle in the oil, beating until thick and creamy. Makes about 1 cup. Chill and serve alongside the bean salad.

# Sunrise Salad

3 cups small shell pasta
(uncooked)
1 large yellow (banana) pepper,
diced
1 onion, diced
2 apples, diced
1 teaspoon dry mustard
½ teaspoon turmeric
1 clove garlic, crushed
¼ cup safflower oil
1 cup cider vinegar
pinch mixed dried herbs
bunch mixed fresh herbs for
garnish

Bring a large saucepan of water to the boil and sprinkle in the pasta. Boil until just tender, rinse in cold water and drain well. Cover and allow to stand for two hours before mixing with other ingredients.

Mix pepper, onion and apples, (red skinned preferably), with the pasta. Combine mustard and turmeric with garlic then beat in the remaining ingredients. Spoon over salad, mixing ingredients carefully to coat well.

Turn into a serving dish. Refrigerate until ready to serve. Garnish with fresh herbs.

# Mt Orange Souffle

8 egg yolks
1¼ cups sugar
2 tablespoons gelatine
1 cup + 2 tablespoons fresh
orange juice
2 tablespoons orange flavoured
liqueur
4 egg whites
1¼ cups cream

Beat egg yolks and half the sugar until creamy. Soften gelatine in the 2 tablespoons orange juice — warm gently to dissolve. Add to the yolks.

Heat over hot water in a double boiler, stirring slowly, until mixture coats the back of a spoon.

Remove from heat — stir in strained orange juice and liqueur. Transfer mixture to a bowl and chill 30 minutes until syrupy.

Whip egg whites until stiff, gradually adding the remaining sugar. Fold in orange mixture.

Whip cream until thick — fold into mixture. Pour into a suitable mould which has been rinsed with cold water. Try to choose a conical or tapered shape. Individual moulds can be used. Chill thoroughly, allowing at least a day for mixture to set. This mixture may also be frozen. To serve, allow to thaw out of mould in refrigerator for 15 minutes before serving. Dust with grated nutmeg.

Accompaniment;
6–8 kiwifruit
3 tablespoons finely chopped
crystallised ginger
2 tablespoons raw sugar

Peel and slice fruit into a bowl. Sprinkle with ginger and sugar and stand at least 30 minutes before serving.

# A BUFFET

## FENNEL SOUP

## TRIPLE CROWN ROAST OF LAMB

## RATATOUILLE

## WATERMELON AND MINT

## WHEAT WITH PARSLEY

## MERINGUE CASE WITH BERRIES

A magnificent sight is a triple crown of lamb adorning the buffet. It may be served hot or cold, but is best when the lamb is a little pink inside. There is one hot dish to stimulate taste buds — the fennel soup starter. If fennel is not in season, then celery could be substituted for the fennel and two teaspoons of fennel seed.

Ratatouille is a traditional favourite — it is a good accompaniment for lamb, and is good hot or cold. Although two tasty salad recipes are given here, cooked, hot, seasonal vegetables can be served instead, if temperatures are low. Warming dishes, hot plates or chafing dishes could be used to help keep the vegetables warm.

Another showstopper is the meringue case, which may be baked ahead and stored in an airtight tin. Fill with berries about an hour before serving — the berries will soften the meringue enough to make cutting easy.

# FENNEL SOUP

750g (1½lb) fennel bulb
750g (1½lb) potatoes
50g (2oz) butter
2 tablespoons oil
2½ litres (quarts) chicken stock
½ teaspoon white pepper

The incorporation of potato into this soup, softens the pungent fennel flavour.

Remove core from fennel and slice. Reserve some sprigs for garnish. Peel potatoes and chop coarsely.

Heat butter and oil in a large heavy saucepan over low heat. Add fennel and potatoes and sauté 10 minutes. Add chicken stock and simmer, partially covered for 30 minutes.

Purée in blender or food processor. Add pepper. Serve in a tureen, soup bowls or mugs. This can be accompanied by crisp, hot, French bread.

# TRIPLE CROWN ROAST OF LAMB

3 crown roasts of diminishing sizes
red currant jelly

Ask your butcher to help prepare this. The base can be prepared from 2 loins of lamb which have been trimmed and chined in a similar way as for a rack of lamb (pg 20). Sew or tie ends together to form a crown. There should be about 18 chops in this first crown. Two smaller crowns need to be prepared, consisting of about 12 and 6 chops respectively. Use smaller chops for the top two crowns. The size of the chops will dictate the number to be used.

Place all three roasts in a large pan. The centres can be supported with empty food cans or a stuffing may be made for the large crown. (Use 4 cups fresh breadcrumbs, 1 sautéd onion, 1 beaten egg, ½ cup chopped parsley and a teaspoon mixed herbs.)

Place fairly low in the oven, protecting the bones from burning with a small piece of foil. Brush with warmed red currant jelly.

Roast 190°C (375°F) for 35 minutes. The meat should be brown on outside and pink inside (cook a further 40 minutes for meat with stuffing). Remove foil during last 5 minutes of cooking.

This can be served hot or allowed to cool and be served chilled and glazed with more jelly. To construct the crown, place middle sized crown into centre of large crown, so it is supported about a third of the way down by the meat. Top with the smallest crown. Place on a large platter. The meat is easily carved between each bone. Start at the top.

Garnish top of bones with paper or foil frills.

# RATATOUILLE

⅓ cup mild olive oil
1 large onion
2 cloves garlic
4 green peppers
4 cups diced eggplant
4 zucchini
6–8 tomatoes
salt and pepper
1 tablespoon olive oil (extra)

Heat oil in a deep heavy saucepan. Slice onions thinly; chop garlic; slice peppers into julienne strips; cut eggplant into 1cm (½in) cubes; slice zucchini into 1cm (½in) pieces; peel, quarter and deseed the tomatoes. About 4 cups of both zucchini and tomatoes should result.

Sauté onion and garlic in oil until golden. Remove from pan. Place layers of the vegetables into the casserole, combining the onion and garlic as well. Sprinkle each layer lightly with salt and pepper. Sprinkle top with the extra olive oil.

Cover and simmer over very low heat for 50 minutes. Press mixture down with a spatula during cooking so juices rise to cover top. Uncover and continue to heat for about 10 minutes until liquid is reduced. Serve hot if lamb is to be served hot, or cold if lamb is to be served chilled. May be refrigerated overnight.

# WATERMELON AND MINT

2kg (4lb) watermelon
1 cup finely chopped mint

Peel and dice watermelon.

Remove any obvious pips from the melon. About 30 minutes before serving, combine with mint and place in a serving bowl.

The melon can also be cut into balls.

# WHEAT WITH PARSLEY

3 cups cracked wheat
1½ cups boiling water
2 cups finely chopped parsley
2 tablespoons chopped fresh
basil or
2 teaspoons dried basil
5 spring onions, finely chopped
2 tomatoes
¾ cup lemon juice
½ cup safflower oil
salt
freshly ground black pepper
4 olives
lettuce leaves

Soak wheat in the water for 1 hour. Drain. Combine with parsley, basil, onion and tomatoes which have been peeled, deseeded and diced. Mix lemon juice with oil and stir into the salad. Season with salt and pepper. Refrigerate for at least an hour before serving. Drain off any excess dressing. Place in a serving bowl and garnish with olives and surround with lettuce.

# MERINGUE CASE WITH BERRIES

¾ cup water
2 cups sugar
6 egg whites
⅛ teaspoon salt

Filling;
8–9 cups fresh berries

Combine sugar and water in a heavy saucepan and bring to boiling point, stirring to dissolve the sugar. Boil syrup until it reaches the soft ball stage, that is 115°C (240°F). This could take about 25 minutes. Remove from heat quickly if syrup starts to look sugary.

While syrup is boiling, beat egg whites until foamy. Add salt and beat until stiff peaks form.

When syrup has reached the soft ball stage, turn the electric mixer on top speed. Slowly pour hot syrup into egg whites in a thin, steady stream. When all syrup has been incorporated, turn mixer to medium speed and continue beating for 10 minutes until mixture is cold. Reserve ¾ cup meringue mixture.

To make meringue case, draw 12 equal circles about 17cm (5in) on two oven trays lined with non-stick baking paper.

Place meringue mixture into a piping bag. Using a plain nozzle, pipe a solid base by making a circle and then filling it with concentric circles until base is filled. Pipe single circles on the other marked places. If trays are not large enough to hold all circles, pipe some double layers of meringue.

Bake at 80°C (175°F) for about 2 hours until circles have dried out and are crisp. Keep remaining mixture in a cool place — this is to be used to cement the circles together.

Place baked circles on top of the base, using a little uncooked meringue to help them stick in place. Cover the inside with meringue. Bake again at a similar temperature for another 2 hours. Allow to cool, before filling with berries. Serve with whipped cream flavoured with an almond liqueur. To serve the cake try to prise off each circle, one per person. Cut double ones in half.

## HOW TO MAKE A MERINGUE CASE

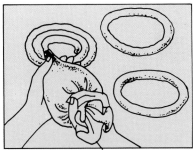

1. Pipe 10–12 circles onto a paper-lined tray, filling one with concentric circles for a base. Bake.

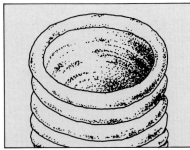

2. Place baked circles on top of base cementing with reserved, uncooked meringue.

3. Cover inside walls with meringue and bake until dry.

## ENTERTAINING TWENTYFOUR

### SESAME CHICKEN
### PAELLA VARIATION

### STRAWBERRIES AND MUSHROOMS
### GREEN AND WHITE SALAD
### LETTUCE WITH CRIMSON CENTRE

### APRICOT PIZZA

This buffet dinner combines a variety of flavours and colours. The main course dishes are served hot. Keep warm if possible on hostess hot plates or over candle burners. If need be, the sesame chicken can be served cold. An improvisation on Mediterranean paella combines shellfish, rice and a tasty sausage — this dish is best prepared in a frypan shortly before serving. (Paella gets its name from the dish it is actually cooked in, a 'paerella', similar to a large frypan.) The chicken can marinate for several hours and is cooked in the oven. If wished, the chicken could be served as a finger food starter — provide guests with paper serviettes to hold the chicken.

The accompaniments are salads — the potato and green pea salad is rich but appealing. Mushrooms and strawberries as a salad are an unusual combination — if raspberry vinegar is unavailable for the dressing, cider vinegar can substitute. Lettuce is given a new look with a raw beetroot filling.

A variation on the savoury pizza is a different dessert. A yeast base with an apricot topping. Fresh apricots are recommended but preserved ones could be used. If they are sweetened then less sugar should be used in the recipe. Serve with whipped cream or a plain yoghurt.

# SESAME CHICKEN

24 chicken drumsticks and/or
24 chicken wings
½ cup sesame seeds

Marinade;
2½ cups dry white wine
1 cup liquid honey
4 cloves garlic
1 cup soy sauce

If chicken is to be served as a starter, then small drumsticks are best. Depending on the age and appetites of your guests, wings and/or drumsticks may be served.

Place chicken in a wide, deep bowl. Combine wine and honey. Warm slightly to dissolve honey. Cool. Mix in garlic and soy sauce. Pour the marinade over the chicken making sure that it is well coated. Marinate overnight, turning occasionally.

To cook, place a selection of chicken on a rack in a large roasting pan. Preferably, cook the chicken in two batches. Place in a hot oven, 200°C (400°F), about 25 minutes for wings and 35 for drumsticks. Brush with marinade during cooking. Place on a platter and keep warm while cooking remaining chicken. Or serve at room temperature.

Sprinkle with sesame seeds before serving.

# PAELLA VARIATION

¼ cup oil
4 onions, chopped
3 cloves garlic, crushed
1 green pepper
1 red pepper
4 cups long grain rice
2 litres (2 quarts) chicken stock
2 large tomatoes, peeled and diced
½ teaspoon ground saffron
4 chorizo sausages
750g (1½lb) cooked prawns
750g (1½lb) steamed mussels
1 green pepper, extra
1 red pepper, extra
salt and pepper
8 cooked prawns in shells
8 small mussels in shells
2 lemons

Heat oil in a very large frypan or 2 smaller frypans. Sauté chopped onion, crushed garlic, and diced peppers until onion is soft. Sprinkle in the rice and fry 1 minute. Pour in boiling chicken stock, tomatoes and saffron.

Bring to the boil, lower heat until just simmering. Arrange sausage, sliced in 1cm (½in) pieces, on top of the rice. Cover and cook on low without stirring, for about 15 minutes or until rice has absorbed all the stock. Add prawns and mussels, plus extra peppers which have been cut into julienne pieces, salt and pepper. Steam a further 10 minutes.

Remove lid and garnish with shellfish in shells, and lemon wedges.

# STRAWBERRIES AND MUSHROOMS

750g (1½lb) button mushrooms
750g (1½lb) small strawberries
¾ cup fruit vinegar
(e.g. raspberry)
½ cup safflower oil
salt and pepper

Wash and dry mushrooms and berries. Remove sepals from strawberries. Combine dressing ingredients well.

30 minutes before serving, pour dressing over mixed salad ingredients. Marinate until just ready to serve. Drain and pile into a salad plate. If strawberries are out of season, peeled and sliced tamarillos can be substituted.

# GREEN AND WHITE SALAD

1 kg (2 lb) frozen peas
1.5 kg (3 lb) peeled potatoes
1 cup French dressing
2 stalks celery, diced
4 spring onions, chopped
1½ cups mayonnaise
1 cup sour cream
1 tablespoon prepared mustard

Bring peas to the boil, cook 1 minute, drain and allow to cool.

Cook potatoes in boiling water until just tender. Cut into 2cm (¾in) dice while still warm. Place in a bowl and carefully mix with French dressing. Stand for 2 hours then add celery, onions and peas.

Combine mayonnaise, sour cream and mustard until smooth. Fold into vegetable mixture carefully. Spoon into a serving dish or mould and refrigerate until ready to serve. If in a mould, dip container in warm water and invert onto a serving plate. Garnish with seasonal greens.

# LETTUCE WITH CRIMSON CENTRE

2 large lettuces
5 medium beetroot
500g (1 lb) red cabbage
2 large carrots, shredded
¾ cup cider vinegar
¼ cup sugar
¼ cup oil
salt and pepper

Choose lettuces with firm hearts. Carefully snip centres from lettuces, leaving an outside shell to hold beetroot mixture. Place lettuces on serving plates. Keep cool.

Wash beetroot and peel if skins are tough. Shred finely into a bowl. Add finely shredded cabbage and carrot.

Heat vinegar and sugar until sugar is dissolved. Cool. Beat in oil. Pour over beetroot mixture and chill. Just before serving, drain off excess dressing and spoon beetroot into the centres of the lettuces. Sprinkle with salt and pepper.

# APRICOT PIZZA

Base:
3 teaspoons dried yeast
2 cups warm water
3 tablespoons sugar
5¾ cups flour
⅛ teaspoon salt
4 tablespoons oil

White flour may be used for the base, or a mixture half white and half wholemeal.

Sprinkle yeast over the water in a bowl. Leave for 2 minutes then stir in the sugar. Stand in a warm place until mixture starts bubbling.

Place flour, salt and oil in a large bowl. Stir in yeast mixture and mix well (use the dough hook on the electric mixer if possible). Knead lightly until shiny. Place in a greased bowl, cover with plastic film and leave in a warm place until double in bulk, 1–2 hours. Remove from bowl and divide dough in half. Pat out dough to fit 3 large, 30cm (12 in) pizza trays or similar.

Filling:
50g (2oz) butter, melted
2.5kg (5lb) fresh apricots
½ cup brown sugar

Brush melted butter over pizza base.

Halve apricots and remove stones. Place cut side up on pizza base making sure base is well covered. Sprinkle evenly with brown sugar.

Place pizzas on a low shelf in the oven. Bake (in a preheated oven), 200°C (400°F) for 20 minutes or until base is cooked and apricots are just tender. (One pizza may have to stand in a cool place while the others are being cooked.) Remove from oven and turn grill onto high. Place pizzas under grill to caramelise sugar lightly. Serve warm dusted with icing sugar (they may be reheated), with plenty of whipped cream, flavoured with orange liqueur.

## A PARTY FOR FIFTY

### FRUIT SALAD GLAZED HAM
### VEAL WITH BASIL SAUCE

---

### CHEESE POTATO BAKE
### BLACK BEAN SALAD
### MIXED SPROUT SALAD
### WITH EAST WEST DRESSING
### TOSSED TOMATO SALAD

---

### HONEY AND GINGER ROLL
### WITH CHAMPAGNE FRUIT

---

If much of the food for a large party can be prepared ahead, then this can make the party more enjoyable for all. The basic rule is 'make it simple'. It has been noticed over the years, that the greater variety of food, the more complicated the menu becomes. Guests like to try a little of everything that is presented. Therefore this menu recommends two cold meat dishes, one only hot (potato) dish and three salads.

Instead of placing all food on the table at once, each salad may be divided between two or three bowls which can be removed when empty and replaced with full dishes. This prevents the dishes from becoming sad and unattractive after several helpings have been removed.

The ham should be glazed on the day, but the veal, potato, black bean salad and honey roll may all be prepared at least a day ahead.

Make a check-list of cutlery, plates and serving dishes well in advance.

# FRUIT SALAD GLAZED HAM

1 x 8kg (16lb) cooked ham on the bone
seasonal fruit; e.g.
6 firm kiwifruit
6 firm red tamarillos

Glaze;
2 tablespoons powdered gelatine or vegetable based setting agent
¼ cup strained orange juice
¾ cup water

1 cup strained and warmed apricot jam could be used as the glaze for this ham in place of the gelatine-based glaze.

With a sharp knife, carefully remove skin from ham, leaving about 10cm (4in) around shank end on which to attach a paper frill.

Peel fruit and slice. Place in layers slightly overlapping each slice, to cover entire top of ham.

Soak gelatine in fruit juice, then dissolve in boiling water. Allow to set until it reaches an egg white consistency. Brush over the fruit, building up a thin layer of glaze over the top. Allow glaze to set before applying a second layer. Attach frill to shank, securing with a pin or toothpick.

COOKING A HAM;

If a cooked ham is not available for the above recipe, here is a recipe for cooking a raw one.

Place raw ham in a roasting dish with 2 cups water and an onion studded with 4 cloves. Cover tightly with foil and bake at 160°C (325°F) for 20 minutes per 500g (1lb). Allow to cool slightly before removing skin. Ham should be completely cold before glazing with fruit as above.

# VEAL WITH BASIL SAUCE

4kg (8lb) baby veal
3 anchovy fillets (optional)
2 cloves garlic, slivered
3 cups chicken stock
2 cups dry white wine
2 cups water
2 onions, quartered
2 carrots, chopped
2 sticks celery, chopped
2 bay leaves
6 sprigs parsley
12 peppercorns

Choose baby veal if possible. If this is not available then soak veal in milk for 2 hours to help remove some of the colour.

With the point of a sharp knife, make several deep incisions in veal. Insert 2cm (¾in) pieces of anchovy and garlic. Place veal in a large saucepan and cover with cold water. Bring to the boil and cook over high heat for 1 minute. Drain. Rinse meat under cold water to remove scum. Place in the clean saucepan and add stock, wine, and water to cover. Add seasonings, partly cover pan and bring to boiling point. Reduce heat and simmer for 1¾ hours, until veal is tender, or reaches 70°C (160°F) internal temperature as measured with a meat thermometer. Allow meat to cool in the stock.

Cut meat into thin slices. Layer on a serving platter (or two), brushing each slice as it is placed, with the basil sauce (see recipe). This may be prepared up to 6 hours in advance. Keep covered with plastic film in refrigerator.

Garnish platter with lemon slices, black olives and parsley. Just before serving, brush veal with a little more of the sauce.

Basil Sauce;
3 cups coarsely chopped basil or
3 cups coarsely chopped parsley and
3 tablespoons dried basil
1 teaspoon salt
1 teaspoon black pepper
6 cloves garlic, crushed
¼ cup finely chopped pine nuts
2 cups corn oil
½ cup finely grated Parmesan cheese

Pack cups firmly with herbs when measuring.

Place herbs in a blender or food processor fitted with a steel blade. Blend until finely chopped. Add seasonings and nuts then, with blender running, gradually pour in oil in a thin stream. Add cheese. Mixture should be thin enough to paint easily over the veal.

# CHEESE POTATO BAKE

400g (14oz) butter
8 medium onions, thinly sliced
8 cloves garlic, crushed
4kg (8lb) peeled potatoes
4 cups evaporated milk
salt and pepper
1 cup finely grated cheddar
cheese

Melt half the butter in a large frypan and sauté onions and garlic for 5 minutes.

Slice potatoes thinly, standing in a bowl of cold salted water to prevent discolouration. Drain before using.

Place half of the potato into 3–4 greased baking dishes. Top with onion mixture and cover with remaining potato.

Spoon evaporated milk over the top. Dot with remaining butter and sprinkle with cheese.

Bake 180°C (350°F) for 35 minutes until tender, or if preparing in advance bake 20 minutes, cool, cover with plastic film and refrigerate. Reheat 190°C (375°F) for 20 minutes.

# BLACK BEAN SALAD

4½ cups (approx 650g) dried
black beans
1½ cups cider vinegar
1½ cups sugar
½ cup water
3 medium onions
salt and pepper

Rinse beans in cold water. Place in a large saucepan and cover with water. Slowly bring to boiling point. Simmer 3 minutes. Remove from heat and stand overnight.

Next day, drain, cover with fresh boiling water, bring to the boil and simmer gently 1 hour or until tender. (Beans should be tender but retain their shape.) Drain and cool.

Bring vinegar, sugar and water to the boil, stirring until sugar is dissolved. Cool. Slice onions thinly, stand in icy water until ready to combine with beans.

Pour dressing over beans and onions combined. Season. Refrigerate for 24 hours before using. Stir before serving.

# MIXED SPROUT SALAD WITH EAST WEST DRESSING

5 cups mung bean sprouts
(approx 250g)
5 cups alfalfa sprouts
(approx 150g)
5 cups radish sprouts
(approx 250g)
300g (10½oz) sliced button
mushrooms
2 x 450g (16oz) cans baby
corn, drained
2 avocados, sliced

East West Dressing;
1 cup oil
1 cup cider vinegar
3 tablespoons soy sauce
2 cloves garlic
4 tablespoons finely chopped
root ginger

This salad is prepared in layers. Rinse sprouts and drain well before using. Salad ingredients should be divided in half and prepared in two bowls.

Place mung beans in the base of a salad bowl. Top with a layer of the mushrooms, then a layer of alfalfa sprouts, more mushrooms, then finish with the radish sprouts. Garnish with baby corn and sliced avocado. Spoon over dressing just before serving.

To make dressing place all ingredients into a food processor or blender and mix well.

# TOSSED TOMATO SALAD

2 large lettuces
(about 2kg in total)
2kg (4lb) tomatoes
(cut into eighths)
2 bunches spring onions,
chopped
2 green peppers, sliced
vinaigrette pg 12

Crisp washed lettuces in plastic bag in refrigerator. Tear into salad bowls at last minute and toss with wedges of tomato and onion. Garnish with peppers. Toss with dressing just before serving.

# HONEY AND GINGER ROLL

4 eggs
⅓ cup castor sugar
3 tablespoons liquid honey
½ teaspoon baking soda
1 tablespoon hot water
1 cup flour
1¼ teaspoons cinnamon

Ingredients given are for 1 roll only. Three should be prepared for fifty people. Each roll cuts into 20 slices. Rolls may be filled with the ginger cream and deep frozen for up to 6 weeks.

Beat eggs with an electric beater for 5 minutes – until thick and light. Gradually add sugar, beating until dissolved. Add honey – beat until creamy.

Sift flour and cinnamon three times then lightly fold into egg mixture.

Pour into a lightly greased and paper-lined 25 x 37cm (10 x 14in) lamington tin. Bake 190°C (375°F) for 12–15 minutes. Turn onto waxed paper. Peel off lining paper and trim edges. Roll up with waxed paper inside, rolling from wide edge. When cool, fill with ginger cream.

Ginger cream:
1½ cups cream
2 tablespoons icing sugar
1 tablespoon ginger syrup
¼ cup finely chopped candied
ginger (in syrup)

Whip cream with icing sugar, stir in syrup. Unroll honey roll and spread with cream. Sprinkle with chopped ginger. Roll up once again.

This log may be frozen. Place on a tray and freeze about 1 hour until solid. Remove from tray and place in a plastic bag and seal well. Return to the freezer. To thaw, remove from freezer about 2 hours before required and place on a serving dish in a cool place. Sprinkle with icing sugar before serving.

# CHAMPAGNE FRUIT

5kg (10lb) fruit approx
castor sugar
2 bottles good sparkling white
wine
1 litre (1 quart) cream, whipped

Choose seasonal fruit, or poached peaches are quite suitable.

Slice fruit or prepare as usual and place in a large fruit bowl. Sprinkle with sugar if need be. Just before serving pour over cold sparkling wine. Or allow guests to help themselves. Serve with whipped cream.

Opposite: Honey and Ginger Roll
with Champagne and Fruit.

## Atmosphere

In creating the right atmosphere for dining, the table, flowers, music and lighting all play an important part. The table can be compared to a stage for the food. It influences the action and the mood. A centre piece for the table can be planned as the focal point from which to build the set. A group of candles, a spray of vegetables, a posy of flowers, a collection of fans or pieces of china could be the focus of the set as well as of discussion. Personal artistic tastes should be allowed to flourish. The dinner ware need not always be a set. Sometimes mixing and matching can be more fun. But however creative one can be, there are a few logical rules to follow when dressing the table.

## Colours

Colours should be considerate and co-ordinate where possible with the food, china and table coverings. Subdued lighting is restful to the diner and complementary to the food. Soft music is a background support at dinnertime, the jazz can come later. The centre piece may be the focal point, but do not allow its height to become embarrassing. Glowing candles can be romantic, but not when they dazzle directly into the eyes of the diner. Candles should be lower than the direct glaze of a seated person, or, very much higher. The height of a flower arrangement should also be considered.

## Buffets

For buffet meals, larger bowls of flowers, baskets of fruit or majestic candelabra can be chosen for a central point. Spot lighting can be used to advantage, with music to follow the theme of the menu. Cutlery can be wrapped in colourful serviettes (table napkins) and tied with streaming ribbons. Buffets may be served from chiffoniers, round or rectangular tables or a series of smaller tables.

## Food

But the most important part of the play is the food, and its presentation has been respected throughout this book. Fresh bright foods, attractively and simply arranged with imagination, with thought to taste, colour and texture – this is the plot which should be supported and enhanced by the table dressing.

## Rules

Traditional these may be, but sometimes the rules have to be modified to suit the situation or style of meal. They should be used as a guideline, not a barrier to ingenuity.

## Cutlery

It is usual to place forks to the left of the placemat or setting, with spoons and knives to the right. Cutting edges of knives should face inwards. Service plates can be used to hold starter and dinner plates. These need not necessarily match the dinner set.

Cutlery to be used first is placed farthest from the plate. For example the soup spoon is placed on the outside right of the plate, the bread-and-butter or starter knife on the inside of this, and the main course knife closest to the plate. It is often easier to have no more than 3 pieces of cutlery at either side. Line the handles about 2.5cm (1in) from the edge of the table.

If necessary, dessert spoons and forks can be placed on the table after the main course. It gives one an opportunity to wash cutlery used previously to provide sufficient for the dessert course.

## Glasses

Water and wine glasses are placed at the tip of the knife and, logically, glasses are filled from the right. Food is served from the left if possible, and empty plates are removed from the right. Coffee is served from the right, the cups being placed at the tip of the dessert spoon. Handles should turn to the right, with the coffee spoon lying at right angles to the cup handle.

A pause between the main course and serving dessert provides an opportunity to clear away condiments and brush the table clear of crumbs. A clean serviette can be used to brush crumbs into a service plate. Bowls of nuts or sweetmeats may be brought to the table to accompany the dessert. Clean glasses and coffee cups may also be presented.

## Seating

Seating requires considerable thought. Usually, the female guest of honour sits on the right of the host but it may be more appropriate to seat a family member beside the host to help with wine or table service. Thought should be given not only to where guests are positioned, but to the space they have in which to move. There should be plenty of elbow room and the table should be sufficiently uncluttered with utensils and people to avoid confusion. Even a best friend can become uncomfortable to find he is eating his neighbour's salad.

## Side tables

If the table is crowded, small side tables or a wagon can be used to hold serving dishes. If the table is large, then it is often easier to provide several smaller platters or casseroles at either end of the table so that service responsibilities are divided. Foods also keep warmer in smaller casseroles. Ideally, a hostess trolley can be set up close by, but candle burners can also be used to keep foods warm. These can be placed on side tables.

Whatever the meal, there is one important rule and that is to serve hot foods hot, and cold foods cold.

## Artichoke

*(Refer chapter, `Flower Food')*

1. Fold the 4 corners of a serviette into the centre. Use a cloth serviette approximately 46cm (18in) square.

2. The serviette forms a square.

3. Repeat step 1.

4. Repeat step 1 again.

5. Turn the serviette over carefully.

6. Repeat step 1.

7. Place a small bowl (or glass) in the centre of the serviette to hold in place.

8. Holding the bowl, pull out the 4 corners.

9. Now pull out from underneath the flaps between the corners.

10. Pull out the remaining corners under the points, giving them a gentle tug. Remove the bowl.

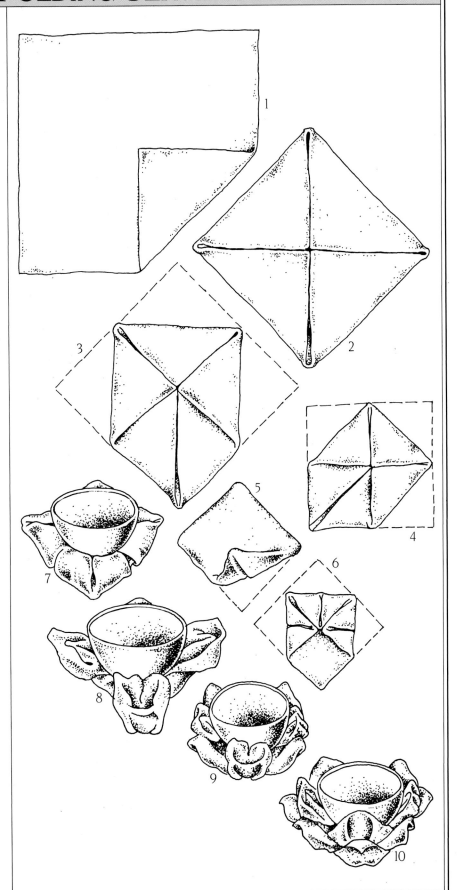

## Triple Fold

*(Refer chapter, 'Light Cooking')*

1. Fold the serviette into quarters. Cloth or heavy paper serviettes may be used, measuring about 38cm (15in) square.

2. Place the serviette with the free corners to the right top. Roll down the top layer to just past the centre.

3. Fold down the next layer and tuck the point under the 1st roll.

4. Fold the 3rd layer under in the opposite direction from the other 2 to form 3 equal bands.

5. Fold under the right and left sides.

6. The serviette is completed. A flower or name place card may be tucked inside the folds.

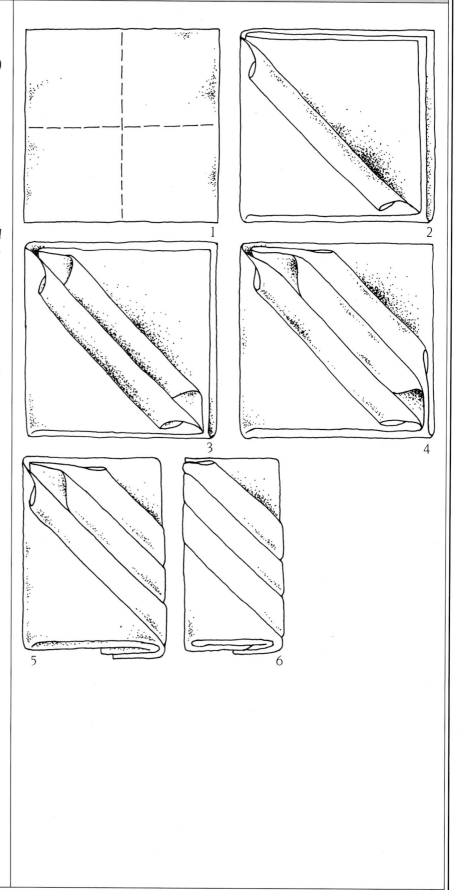

## Temple Bells

1. Fold serviette in half diagonally. Use a stiff cloth or heavy paper serviette measuring approximately 38cm (15in) square.

2. Place fold at the bottom.

3. Place a finger at the centre of the bottom edge, fold up the left and right points straight with the centre point.

4. Fold up bottom point about 10cm (4in).

5. Return point to touch bottom edge.

6. Fold in the points 2.5cm (1in) in accordian-type pleats.

7. Place folded serviette into a glass, keeping the bottom point outside the glass. Pull sides out and down.

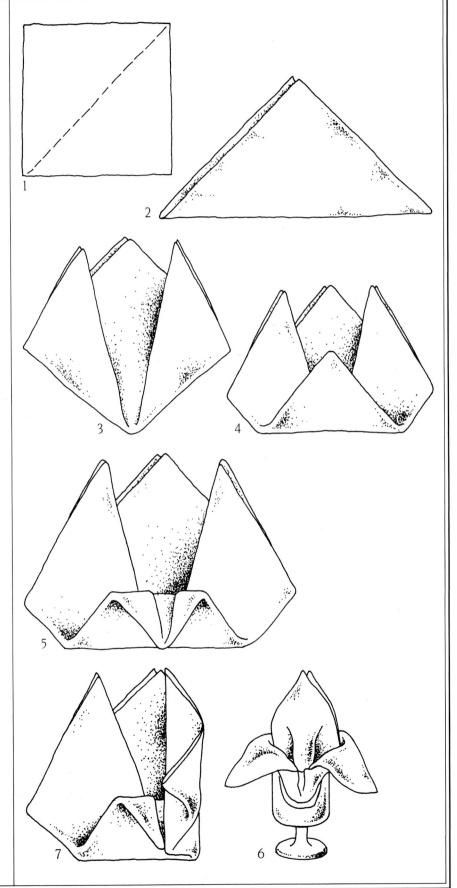

## For Buffets

*(Refer chapter, 'A Party for Fifty')*

1. Start with the outline of arrangement to set height and width. The backbone should be as upright as possible. Place to the back of container in well soaked oasis (floral foam). Then place sidesprays in position.

2. Fill in outline of arrangement, camouflaging oasis (floral foam) well.

3. Add extra flowers, grading them down in size into centre of the arrangement, and continue a gentle flow to the sides.

4. The centre of the arrangement is the most important and should hold the largest flowers.

# FLOWER ARRANGEMENTS

## Central Posy Bowl

(Refer chapter, 'The Good Things In Life')

1. Place oasis (floral foam) in low round bowl and secure with wire. Soak well.

2. Cut 2 stems about 18cm (7in) each and place on outer edge opposite each other, keeping parallel with each other.

3. Cut 2 stems slightly shorter and place opposite each other at right angles to first stems. Support these 4 stems with shorter stems keeping a low line.

4. Complete one side by adding full blooms and extra foliage. Complete the other side in a similar way. The height should be no more than 15cm (6in).

The table itself affects the line. Rectangular tables require a 2 sided horizontal line whereas a round or oval table suggests a circle based design.

# VEGETABLE GARNISHES

## HOW TO MAKE RADISH FLOWERS AND SPRING ONION CURLS

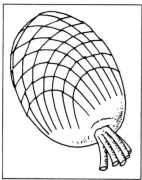  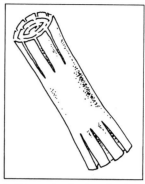 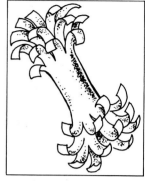

(Refer Spinach Salad)
1. Trim radish. Using a sharp knife make parallel cuts close together from the top of the radish to within 3mm (⅛in) of the stem end.

2. Turn radish at a 90° angle and make an equal number of cuts perpendicular to the first ones. Soak in icy water to open the flower.

1. Trim ends of onion. Cut into approximately 8cm (3in) lengths. Using a sharp knife make slashes in one or both ends.

2. Soak in icy water to curl ends.

## HOW TO MAKE CELERY CURLS AND GREEN PEPPER FANS

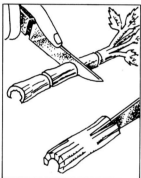 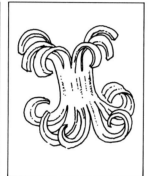 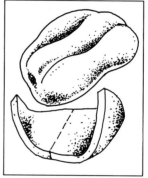 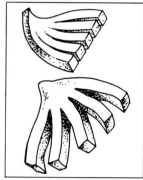

(Refer Pork in Orange Sauce)
1. Cut celery sticks into 5–8cm (2–3in) lengths. Cut lengthwise into halves or quarters.

2. Finely slash one or both ends of sticks. Stand in icy water to curl.

(Refer Tropical Salad Plate)
1. Cut a green pepper in half lengthwise, removing seeds and ribs. Cut in quarters then each quarter in half.

2. Make 4 evenly spaced cuts in the broad end of each fan and soak in icy water until fan opens.

## HOW TO MAKE A CROUTON CASE

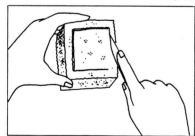  

(Refer Croûton with Stir-fry)
1. Start with 2 loaves of white bread. Remove crusts. Cut into 8cm (3in) cubes.

2. With a sharp knife cut 2cm (¾in) inside the cube along 4 sides. Cut to within 1cm (½in) of the base. Remove bread from centre with a teaspoon.

3. Brush case with melted butter. Bake 160° (325°F) for about 12 minutes until golden.

114

# WEIGHTS AND MEASURES

Standard metric weights and measures are used throughout this book. A good set of scales, a graduated measuring cup and set of standard metric spoons is useful.

Note: for successful cooking use either metric weights or measures, or, imperial weights and measures – do not mix the two.

In many recipes, imperial equivalents of metric measures are shown in brackets. For example 500g (1lb) beef. Although the metric yield of a cup is about 10% greater, the proportions remain the same.

## Cup and spoon measures

| metric | approx. |
|---|---|
| ¼ cup | 60ml |
| ½ cup | 125ml |
| 1 cup | 250ml |
| 4 cups | 1000ml or 1 litre |
| | |
| 1 teaspoon | 5ml |
| 1 dessertspoon | 10ml |
| 1 tablespoon | 15ml |

## Abbreviations

| | | |
|---|---|---|
| g | = | gram |
| kg | = | kilogram |
| mm | = | millimetre |
| cm | = | centimetre |
| ml | = | millilitre |
| °C | = | degree Celsius |
| °F | = | degree Fahrenheit |
| in | = | inch |
| lb | = | pound |
| oz | = | ounce |

## Grams to ounces

These are converted to the nearest round number.

| grams | | ounces |
|---|---|---|
| 25 | = | 1 |
| 50 | = | 2 |
| 75 | = | 3 |
| 100 | = | 3½ |
| 125 | = | 4 |
| 150 | = | 5 |
| 175 | = | 6 |
| 200 | = | 7 |
| 225 | = | 8 |
| 250 | = | 9 |
| 275 | = | 10 |
| 300 | = | 10½ |
| 325 | = | 11 |
| 350 | = | 12 |
| 375 | = | 13 |
| 400 | = | 14 |
| 425 | = | 15 |
| 450 | = | 16 (1lb) |
| 1kg | = 1000g = | 2lb 4oz |

## Measures of length

| cm | | approx. inches |
|---|---|---|
| 0.5 (or 5mm) | = | ¼ |
| 1 | = | ½ |
| 2.5 | = | 1 |
| 5 | = | 2 |
| 15 | = | 6 |
| 18 | = | 7 |
| 20 | = | 8 |
| 23 | = | 9 |
| 25 | = | 10 |
| 30 | = | 12 |

## Oven setting equivalents (to nearest 10°C)

| | Fahrenheit | Celsius | Gas regulo no. |
|---|---|---|---|
| very cool | 225–275 | 110–140 | ¼–1 |
| cool | 300–325 | 150–160 | 2–3 |
| moderate | 350–375 | 180–190 | 4–5 |
| hot | 400–425 | 200–240 | 6–8 |
| very hot | 475–500 | 250–260 | 9–10 |

# GLOSSARY

| | |
|---|---|
| beetroot | beets |
| eggplant | aubergine |
| sweet potato | kumara, yam |
| minced (beef) | ground |
| schnitzel | escalope, scallopine or cutlet |
| prawn | shrimp |
| squid | calamari |
| baking soda | bicarbonate of soda |
| cornflour | cornstarch |
| caster/castor sugar | powdered or superfine granulated |
| icing sugar | confectioners' |
| flour | all purpose flour |
| wholemeal flour | wholewheat flour |
| essence (rose) | extract |

| | |
|---|---|
| mixed spice | mixture of powdered cloves, nutmeg, cinnamon or ginger |
| cooking chocolate | baking semi-sweet chocolate |
| ghee | clarified butter |
| cottage cheese | ricotta cheese |
| sultanas | raisins |
| kibbled or cracked wheat | burghul or bulgur |
| jumbalaya | mixture of seafood |
| cobb/cob loaf | round loaf bread |
| tasty cheese | sharp cheese |
| tomato sauce (condiment) | ketchup, catsup |
| tomato purée | tomato sauce (U.S.A.) |
| serviette | dinner napkin |

*Smoked Salmon with Dill Dressing. (Refer pg12)*

Thank you,

Milne's of Remuera
320 Remuera Road, Auckland
for supplying cutlery, china and glassware for photography

G.R. Newgoods
importers
for arranging the Mikasa dinnerware and cutlery for photography

also
Gibsons and Patterson
Airest Furniture
Jenny Hames, (flowers)
Anne Tinson, (catering assistance)
Susan Gee, (prop assistant)

# INDEX

# INDEX

# INDEX